THE INCREDIBLE COVER-UP

ii

Are you going up in the rapture? Is it true that thousands of people will suddenly disappear one day — soon? Will you be left behind? Will the greatest series of disasters ever known to man begin to occur shortly thereafter? Is Hal Lindsey, author of *The Late Great Planet Earth*, right when he says that the rapture will come before that great end-time tribulation? Will there be a "pre-trib rapture"?

Dave MacPherson has done important research into the origin and effects of this belief in a "pre-trib rapture." His task took him to England and Scotland and finally focused on the ship-building city of Port Glasgow. In places his report reads like a detective story and what he finally tells is both fascinating and surprising.

Christian Life (May, 1974) said, it "will intrigue you . . . it might even make you angry."

Christianity Today (February 1, 1974) called it a "staunch defense."

Moody Monthly (September, 1974) said it was "careful, factual, sleuthing . . . well worth acquiring. . . ."

Harold Ockenga, the President of Gordon College and Seminary, said, "Apparently you have uncovered a very illuminating fact" (in a letter to the author).

Arthur Katterjohn of Wheaton College calls it "a fascinating book written in a light, readable style."

Harry Conn, President of Men for Missions, says of this book, ". . . For the good of God's people, it must have a good circulation."

This book will, incidentally, absorb students of the life of Edward Irving and the Catholic Apostolic Church — subjects introduced by Larry Christenson in his *Message to the Charismatic Movement.*

About the author — Dave MacPherson, seen above standing before the old Town Hall of Port Glasgow, Scotland, studied at Wheaton College and earned his bachelor's degree from Long Beach State College in California. Articles by him have appeared in more than a hundred different publications. A newsman, he lives with his wife and family in Kansas City, Missouri, where he works in Christian radio.

THE INCREDIBLE COVER-UP

Exposing the Origins of Rapture Theories

Dave MacPherson

OMEGA PUBLICATIONS
MEDFORD, OREGON

International Standard Book Number: 0-931608-06-6 (softcover)
Library of Congress Catalog Number: 75-25171
Printed and bound in the United States

Second Printing—August, 1980
Third Printing—July, 1991
Fourth Printing—December, 1993
Fifth Printing—August, 1995
Sixth Printing—July, 1996
Seventh Printing—May, 1999
Eighth Printing—November, 2001
THE INCREDIBLE COVER-UP

All rights transferred to:
Omega Publications
P.O. Box 4130
Medford, Oregon 97501

v

FOREWORD

By Dr. James McKeever

PLEASE BE SURE TO READ THIS FOREWORD *BEFORE* YOU READ THIS BOOK

Cover-ups make people angry. In fact, the Watergate cover-up made our entire Congress and even our entire nation angry.

Dave MacPherson, researcher and journalist, started to investigate the origin of the pre-tribulation rapture theory. His task took him to England and Scotland, where he talked with people and visited many libraries and research facilities. He discovered what he feels to be a cover-up of the origin and basis of this widely-accepted doctrine. The cover-up made him angry.

Some of his anger shows through in this book. At times he speaks harshly of those he feels are responsible for the conception and perpetration of this cover-up. However, I am convinced that Dave loves these other brothers in Christ, even though he may not agree with them on some theological points, such as the timing of the rapture.

Dave knows Jesus Christ as his savior and has a heart to help Christians. He realizes that, as Christians, our fellowship is around the beautiful Person of Jesus Christ, and that as long as a brother is preaching Jesus Christ as the Son of God and the only way to heaven, we can have sweet fellowship together, regardless of whether we agree on different peripheral issues such as baptism, the Holy Spirit, or the rapture.

Omega Publications is continuing the printing of this book because of the valuable information and research contained in it. J. Barton Payne in the *Journal of the Evangelical Theological Society*, says it is "the most in-depth study yet to be made available on the origins of pretribulationism . . . the study of MacPherson's discoveries has become a must."

Most Christians who believe in a rapture at the beginning of the tribulation do not know how this theological belief came into existence or what their biblical basis is for believing it. They have simply been taught it by teachers they respect, and therefore have accepted it, without doing personal research into the origins and the biblical basis of the pretribulation rapture theory. It would seem wise for Christians who hold this position to examine its foundations with an open mind, asking the Spirit of the Living God to either confirm their existing beliefs or to show them what they should believe differently.

My prayer for you is that God will guide you into His perfect truth about the end-times events, but above all that you would love Him with all of your heart, soul, mind and strength. If you love Him in this way, your entire Christian life will fall properly into place. We love Him because He first loved us. He demonstrated how much He loved us in that He was willing to send His Son, Jesus Christ, to die in our place, that believing in Him we might have eternal life.

As this world races toward the climax of this age, the anchor that we have is God, His Son, and His truth. May this book help you gain a better understanding of the truth of God and may it be an enlightenment to you.

Yours to the glory of God and His Son Jesus,

James McKeever

CONTENTS

ACKNOWLEDGMENTS

Quotations from *A History of the Brethren Movement* by F. Roy Coad, Copyright © 1968 The Paternoster Press; *The Basis of Millennial Faith* by Floyd Hamilton, Copyright 1942 by Wm. B. Eerdmans Publishing Co.; *The Millennium in the Church* by D. H. Kromminga, Copyright 1945 by Wm. B. Eerdmans Publishing Co.; *Crucial Questions About the Kingdom of God*, Copyright 1952 by Wm. B. Eerdmans Publishing Co., and *The Blessed Hope*, Copyright 1956 by Wm. B. Eerdmans Publishing Co., by George E. Ladd; and *The Imminent Appearing of Christ* by J. Barton Payne, © Copyright 1962 Wm. B. Eerdmans Publishing Co., are used by permission of Wm. B. Eerdmans Publishing Co.

Quotation from *A History of the Plymouth Brethren* by William B. Neatby is used by permission of Hodder and Stoughton Ltd.

Quotations from *Re-Thinking the Rapture* by E. Schuyler English, Copyright 1954 by E. Schuyler English, and *Not Wrath, But Rapture* by H. A. Ironside and *The Basis of the Premillennial Faith* by Charles C. Ryrie, Copyright 1953 by Loizeaux Brothers, Inc., are used by permission of Loizeaux Brothers, Inc.

Quotations from *The Origins of the Brethren* by Harold H. Rowdon, Copyright © 1967 by Harold H. Rowdon, are used by permission of Pickering & Inglis Ltd.

Quotation from *The Prophetic Faith of Our Fathers* by LeRoy E. Froom, Copyright © 1950 by the Review & Herald Publishing Association, is used by permission of the author and the publisher.

Quotations from *The Puritan Hope* by Iain H. Murray, © Copyright 1971 by Iain H. Murray, are used by permission of The Banner of Truth Trust, Publishers.

Quotation from *Prophecy and the Church* by Oswald T. Allis, Copyright 1945, 1947, by Oswald T. Allis, is used by permission of The Presbyterian and Reformed Publishing Company.

Quotations from *The Roots of Fundamentalism* by Ernest R. Sandeen, © 1970 by The University of Chicago, are used by permission of The University of Chicago Press.

Quotations from *The Late Great Planet Earth* by Hal Lindsey and C. C. Carlson, © 1970 by Zondervan Publishing House; *Things To Come* by J. Dwight Pentecost, Copyright 1958 by Dunham Publishing Company; *Kept From The Hour* by Gerald B. Stanton, Copyright 1956 by Zondervan Publishing House; and *The Rapture Question* by John F. Walvoord, Copyright 1957 by Dunham Publishing Company, are used by permission of Zondervan Publishing House.

. . to my godly parents and wife
who agonized and assisted

PREFACE

Will all true believers in Christ remain on earth during the great tribulation? Or will they be raptured away before that time of trouble? Hal Lindsey's *The Late Great Planet Earth*, pp. 137–138, says this is the big question. Lindsey believes there is a generation of believers that will be removed from earth before the Tribulation begins. He calls this end-time escape the Christian's real hope, the "blessed hope" of believers. This pre-trib rapture is a major theme of his book.

My purpose in writing this book is to examine the incredible *origin and effects* of pre-trib rapture teaching.

All Bible-exalting persons believe in the "catching up" of I Thessalonians 4, but there is still disagreement on the time of this event—chiefly whether it happens before the Tribulation or after.

Since my college days I have been a news reporter, covering fatal car accidents, train disasters, plane crashes, forest fires, and floods. I have filmed tornadoes in action, an atom bomb explosion in Nevada, and many notable people including several U.S. presidents. I have worked for newspapers, TV, and radio, and the past nine years in Christian radio as a mobile unit newsman.

But nothing—absolutely nothing—has ever intrigued me as much as my search into the origin of pre-trib (or two-stage) rapture teaching.

The search really got underway with the discovery in the

fall of 1971 of a rare book in an Illinois bookstore, a book which changed my life and drew exciting reactions from many outstanding Bible scholars around the world.

In 1972 my wife and I flew home from London after an exhaustive time of research in England and Scotland, and the following pages are packed with stunning information gleaned from a variety of sources. I have noted these sources carefully at the end of the book.

I want to express my gratitude to the officials of the British Museum, Edinburgh University Library, Evangelical Library, Mitchell Library, National Library of Scotland, and New College Library, as well as to those in this country at Central Baptist Seminary, Midwestern Baptist Theological Seminary, Nazarene Theological Seminary, and Wheaton College, in addition to other libraries and institutions here and abroad, for permission to prosecute research inside their facilities and to obtain and use photocopied material.

I am indebted to Dr. F. F. Bruce of the University of Manchester for valuable advice and assistance. I also extend thanks to Arthur Katterjohn and Ed F. Sanders of Wheaton College, and to R. L. Nissly of Zionsville, Pennsylvania, all three having helped me in innumerable ways.

Special mention should also be made of the kindness and help of Norman F. Douty of Swengel, Pennsylvania; of George H. Fromow of the Sovereign Grace Advent Testimony in London; and of Jack Green of Hemsworth, Yorkshire, whose aid, hospitality, and devotion to research were much appreciated on both sides of the Atlantic.

This preface would indeed be incomplete if it failed to recognize the many friends of like mind met through the columns of *Logos Journal, Christianity Today, Christian Life*, the Canadian *Inquirer*, and other publications.

Those who materially assisted in this undertaking would most certainly include Mary Brown of Chicago, and William M. Round of Tacoma. In this regard Harry Conn, president of Men for Missions in Minneapolis, must also be acknowledged.

In this life it will never be possible for me to express gratitude to one whose observations and writings comprise the most important portions of this book, for he died ninety-two years ago. His name—Dr. Robert Norton.

DAVE MACPHERSON

PART I

The Unbelievable Pre-Trib Origin

1. INTRODUCTION

"The Second Coming of Christ is in two stages. First He comes *for* the saints and then later He comes back *with* the saints."

"The day of Christ is the first stage and the day of the Lord is the second stage."

"The rapture is the first stage—when Christ comes for the Church. The second stage is when He returns in judgment."

Phrases like these are heard constantly in the United States over Christian radio and TV. A fellow believer from a foreign country quickly gets the idea that American preachers seldom experience "stage" fright, that we get our prophecy in "stages." The foreigner also learns that we take biblical prophecy quite seriously and soon discovers that this topic is more often than not a main ingredient of many broadcasts and telecasts.

If a backwoods preacher suddenly announces that he will soon commence a detailed radio series on the book of Revelation housewives madly change their plans so as not to miss a single exciting segment. If a Christian bookstore has a discount day and is featuring books on prophecy, there is a crowd—especially if the books contain prophetic charts where "you can see everything at a glance."

No wonder some outsiders speak of "the thin mental veneer" they detect here. Too often we seem so engrossed with the future that we brush aside the present and the past. But, like the kid with the red hair, many things have a traceable origin. Fruit does indeed have a root, and if you want to understand the fruit, you must find and look at the root.

Romans 11:16 (ASV) says that "if the root is holy, so are the branches." And it follows that the fruit on such branches is also holy. Sure, we're fruit inspectors. But how many of us are root inspectors?

Being the son and grandson of fervently evangelical author-preachers (they collectively authored several dozen books which are often found in Christian college and seminary libraries), I am no stranger to biblical prophecy.

In my Bible institute days I learned the hard way that there are sharply disagreeing schools of prophetic interpretation. I would discuss prophecy at various times with other students and bring up viewpoints differing in detail from the school's official position.

This finally resulted in my dismissal. This in spite of the fact that the institute president had been my father's classmate years before at Princeton Seminary—during the golden era of Charles R. Erdman, J. Gresham Machen, and Robert Dick Wilson. His action came without warning and I was deeply hurt.

Some Bible schools still make some minor point of prophecy a test of fellowship, although happily their number is rapidly diminishing. Perhaps these schools are finally listening to scholars like Chafer, Ladd, Ryrie, and Walvoord, all of whom have written that Christians should never draw away from other true believers simply because their prophetic beliefs may not coincide point for point.

In any discussion of prophecy it's always good to define the terms used.

The main millennial [1] schools of interpretation: a-millennial, post-millennial, and pre-millennial.

If a person is an *a-mill,* he generally doesn't believe in a future, literal millennium, but he believes that the present age is the time of Christ's reign. Although some see no future tribulation, a significant number of a-mills do see a future time of unparalleled trouble. Regardless of the a-mill's definition of the tribulation, he generally holds to a post-tribulational rapture.

The *post-mill* view resembles the a-mill in a number of ways, except that Christ is seen coming again at the end of the millennium. The tribulation is vague and can be considered as already past, having taken place during the apostolic period possibly. The post-mill generally sees the world getting better and better, with the church itself, instead of Christ, ushering in a time of universal peace. The post-mill necessarily believes in a post-tribulational rapture, no matter how he defines the tribulation.

But it is in the *pre-mill* division that most of the current hyperventilation over the time of the rapture and the church's relationship to the great tribulation seems to take place.

All in this group see Christ's return before the millennium and, roughly speaking, there are four principal divisions of pre-mills: pre-tribulationists, mid-tribulationists, post-tribulationists, and partial rapturists.

Most exponents of these four positions teach a future time of great tribulation followed by the millennium, while some view the tribulation period as present or even past.

The pre-trib sees the rapture before the tribulation, the mid-trib sees it somewhere in the middle, the post-trib at the end of it, and the partial rapturist sees more than one rapture, or a series of raptures, which can take place anywhere from the start to the finish of the period.

All four pre-mill divisions believe in a post-trib coming of Christ when He will come in judgment. But three out of four—pre-tribs, mid-tribs, and partial rapturists—see another coming before the coming in judgment. They call this first coming the rapture. Another name for it would be the translation. This refers to the time when believers are caught up to meet Christ in the air (I Thessalonians 4:17).

Post-tribs teach that the rapture takes place at Christ's

coming in judgment. Other pre-mills, however, are convinced that the rapture is separated from the coming in judgment by an interval of time. Another term for the coming in judgment is the revelation.

Some refer to the two comings as a double coming. Others may term this a split rapture. Still others speak of two phases, or two stages, of the second coming.

Among the four pre-mill groups mentioned, and even among those who are not classified pre-mill, there has been no little debate over the origin of this two-stage teaching, the first stage being the rapture which removes believers from either all or part of the tribulation.

If there are two stages, then a Christian can confidently expect to escape the tribulation, that is, if he believes the tribulation is yet to come.

If, on the other hand, the two-stage teaching is an early nineteenth century invention which first saw the light of day in Great Britain and does not truly reflect the teaching of the New Testament, as some scholars claim, then Christians must seriously begin to ask themselves if God is going to require them to endure suffering for Him in a time of tribulation.

NOTES

1. The Millennium refers to the thousand years of Christ's reign on earth mentioned in Revelation 20.

2. SOME POST SCRIPTS

Some who believe in and teach a post-tribulational rapture maintain that pre-tribulationism is a fairly modern doctrine. They pinpoint the birth of two-stage advent teaching in 1830, sometimes 1832.

Samuel P. Tregelles, an early Brethren scholar, said belief in the secret pre-trib rapture originated about the year 1832 in his book, *The Hope of Christ's Second Coming*, p. 35 (1864). In a footnote on the same page he wrote:

> I am not aware that there was any definite teaching that there would be a *secret* rapture of the Church at a secret coming, until this was given forth as an "utterance" in Mr. Irving's Church, from what was there received as being the voice of the Spirit. But whether any one ever asserted such a thing or not, it was from that supposed revelation that the modern doctrine and the modern phraseology respecting it arose. It came not from Holy Scripture, but from that which falsely pretended to be the Spirit of God, while not owning the true doctrines of our Lord's incarnation in the same flesh and blood as His brethren, but without taint of sin. After the opinion of a secret advent had been adopted, many expressions in older writers were regarded as supporting it; in which, however, the word "secret" does not mean unperceived or unknown, but simply secret in point of time. . . . Sometimes from a hymn being *altered,* writers appear to set forth a secret rapture of which they had never heard, or against which they have protested.

The "Mr. Irving" to whom Tregelles referred was Edward Irving, a leading figure in the formation of the Catholic

Apostolic Church in England in the 1830s. More about him later.

In 1937 Alexander Reese wrote a detailed and much-quoted volume, *The Approaching Advent of Christ.* Many people regard it as a post-trib classic.

In the first chapter he sketches prophetic beliefs held by pre-mills until "the second quarter of the nineteenth century." The entire quote on pages 17–18 is as follows:

> Until the second quarter of the nineteenth century general agreement existed among pre-millennial advocates of our Lord's Coming concerning the main outlines of the prophetic future: amidst differences of opinion on the interpretation of the Apocalypse and other portions of Scripture, the following scheme stood out as fairly representative of the school:—
>
> (1) The approaching Advent of Christ to this world will be visible, personal, and glorious.
>
> (2) This Advent, though in itself a single crisis, will be accompanied and followed by a variety of phenomena bearing upon the history of the Church, of Israel, and the world. Believers who survive till the Advent will be transfigured and translated to meet the approaching Lord, together with the saints raised and changed at the first resurrection. Immediately following this, Antichrist and his allies will be slain, and Israel, the covenant people, will repent and be saved, by looking upon Him whom they pierced.
>
> (3) Thereupon the Messianic Kingdom of prophecy, which, as the Apocalypse informs us, will last for a thousand years, will be established in power and great glory in a transfigured world. The nations will turn to God, war and oppression cease, and righteousness and peace cover the earth.
>
> (4) At the conclusion of the kingly rule of Christ and His saints, the rest of the dead will be raised, the Last Judgement ensue, and a new and eternal world be created.
>
> (5) No distinction was made between the *Coming* of our Lord, and His *Appearing, Revelation,* and *Day,* because these were all held to be synonymous, or at least related, terms, signifying always the one Advent in glory at the beginning of the Messianic Kingdom.

(6) Whilst the Coming of Christ, no matter how long the present dispensation may last, is the true and proper hope of the Church in every generation, it is nevertheless conditioned by the prior fulfilment of certain signs or events in the history of the Kingdom of God: the Gospel has first to be preached to all nations; the Apostasy and the Man of Sin be revealed, and the Great Tribulation come to pass. Then shall the Lord come.

(7) The Church of Christ will not be removed from the earth until the Advent of Christ at the very end of the present Age: the Rapture and the Appearing take place at the same crisis; hence Christians of that generation will be exposed to the final affliction under Antichrist.

Such is a fair statement of the fundamentals of Pre-millennialism as it has obtained since the close of the Apostolic Age. There have been differences of opinion on details and subsidiary points, but the main outline is as I have given it.

On page 227 of the same book Reese is more specific concerning the time of the origin:

Yet the undeniable fact is that this "any-moment" view of Christ's Return only originated about 1830, when Darby gave forth at the same time the mistaken theory of the Secret Coming and Rapture; but all down the centuries there had existed Christians who longed for the Revelation of Christ, whilst expecting that Antichrist would come first.

Reese has some added thoughts on page 240:

All down the centuries the Church expected Christ's Coming after the arrival of Antichrist, according to the teaching of Christ and His Apostles. Only in 1830 did a school arise that treats with intolerance, and often with contempt, the attitude of those who had looked for Him in the manner just named. Not the slightest respect was paid to a view that had held the field for 1,800 years.

Floyd E. Hamilton's *The Basis of Millennial Faith* (1942) also touches upon the commencement of two-stage rapturism. His treatment can be found on pages 23–24:

About a hundred years ago a man named J. N. Darby, founded a group of Christians who have become known as "The

Brethren," or "Plymouth Brethren." His followers, Wm. Kelly, W. Trotter, and C. H. M., were the pioneers of the movement, but in more recent times W. E. Blackstone, in "Jesus is Coming," F. W. Grant, James M. Gray, A. C. Gaebelein, F. C. Ottman, and particularly C. I. Scofield, the author of the "Scofield Reference Bible," have popularized what we may call a new view of the events preceding and following the Coming of Christ. It is important to note that there is a vast difference between the teachings of these men and the teachings of the old historic premillennialists.

Three years after Hamilton's book was published, Oswald T. Allis' *Prophecy and the Church* (1945) spoke briefly of the historical period in question. Allis, a leading scholar, wrote on page 168:

> The Brethren were opposed to Irvingism, but it cannot be denied that, however they came by it, they speedily became ardent advocates of what is called the "any moment" doctrine of the coming.

At the same time there appeared D. H. Kromminga's *The Millennium in the Church* (1945). I quote from page 250:

> Pretribulationism may have other sources also, but no doubt one such source lies in the teaching of Darby.
> That there are other sources of pretribulationism and ultra-dispensationalism becomes clear when we turn our attention to the Catholic Apostolic Church, which came into being at about the same time . . . . In 1830, members of a Presbyterian family near Glasgow began to speak in tongues. This phenomenon was paralleled at London in 1831, and then at Bristol and other places. These prophecies made it plain that the return of the Lord depended upon the proper spiritual preparation of His Church, which preparation included also the restoration of the apostolate.

George E. Ladd, a well-known defender of the post-trib rapture position, shares his knowledge of two-stage beginnings in two of his books. In a footnote included on page 49 in his *Crucial Questions About the Kingdom of God* (1952), Ladd writes:

> It is not important for the present purpose to determine whether the views of Darby and Kelly were original with them or were taken over from their antecedents and made popular by them. Sources to solve this historical problem are not available to the present writer. For all practical purposes, we may consider that this movement—for dispensationalism has had such wide influence that it must be called a movement—had its source with Darby and Kelly.

A later book written by Ladd entitled *The Blessed Hope* (1956), pages 40–41, has additional details:

> It was at Powerscourt that the teaching of a pretribulation rapture of the Church took shape. Tregelles, a member of the Brethren in these early days, tells us that the idea of a secret rapture at a secret coming of Christ had its origin in an "utterance" in Edward Irving's church, and that this was taken to be the voice of the Spirit.

Another prophetic writer of note is J. Barton Payne, who authored *The Imminent Appearing of Christ* (1962). On page 32 in his book Payne says:

> For soon after 1830 a woman, while speaking in tongues, announced the "revelation" that the true church would be caught up (raptured) to heaven before the tribulation and before Christ's return to earth. Irving was deposed from the ministry and died in 1834, but not before his "pre-tribulationism" had been introduced at the Powerscourt meetings.

Payne has more to say on page 156:

> For a brief time at Powerscourt House the troublesome possibility persisted of an eventual involvement of the heavenly (Brethren) church in an earthly tribulation, but then came the "heaven-sent" Irvingite discovery of the secret, pre-tribulational rapture . . . . The pre-tribulational reconstruction was, confessedly an innovation, unsuspected in Biblical interpretation until Irving's "utterance."

The writers quoted above represent only a small fraction of those who have attempted, at one time or another, to track down the birth of two-stage teaching. Going over their remarks, we can see that they agree on certain details:

Irving and a woman's "utterance."

John Darby and the Brethren.

The approximate time of 1830.

A setting somewhere in Great Britain.

Now let's turn our attention to some leaders in the pre-trib camp and see what their reactions are.

3. A FEW REBUTTALS

It is my intention here to give equal time to some of the most knowledgeable and influential pre-trib scholars. As in the preceding chapter, the older writers will have their say first.

At the head of the list is W. E. Blackstone's *Jesus Is Coming* (1878), a favorite pre-trib classic which has been reprinted regularly right to the present day. On page 36 Blackstone penned these words:

> The Church, hand in hand with the world, plunged into the dark ages, until awakened by the great reformers of the sixteenth century, who again began to proclaim the comforting hope and blessed promise of the coming of Christ; and since that time the subject so long neglected has been studied and preached with increasing interest. Indeed, in the last two centuries, it seems to have risen (with the doctrine of salvation by simple faith in a crucified Saviour) into somewhat the same prominence which it occupied in the early church. God be praised for it.

H. A. Ironside went into more detail in *Not Wrath, But Rapture* (n.d.) on pages 43–44:

> Others again have tried to put the stigma of demonism upon the precious truth that the Lord may return at any time to take His saints to be with Himself preceding the great tribulation, endeavoring to link this with certain theories taught by the late Edward Irving and his followers in the early part of the nineteenth century. But any one at all acquainted with Irving's actual teaching can see how truly false this is. From the time when prophetic truth long neglected came again into promi-

nence, there was a great deal of confusion regarding the two aspects of the Lord's return, mentioned above; but eminent Bible teachers who weighed all the scriptures carefully and prayerfully before God, were led little by little to see the distinction between the Church as the Body of Christ and the saints of a coming age who would be witnesses for the Lord in the time of the tribulation, and would share with Him in the manifested kingdom. The more carefully these views have been examined by men of God dependent upon the teaching of the Holy Spirit through the Word, the more they have been seen to be distinctly in harmony with divine revelation.

In 1953 Charles C. Ryrie, in his book *The Basis of the Premillennial Faith* (page 33) wrote:

Certain refinements may be of recent origin, but premillennialism was certainly the faith of the Church centuries before the Brethren and Darby.

Kept From The Hour (1956), by Gerald B. Stanton, has several paragraphs giving his views on the start of pre-trib rapturism. On page 217 he says:

Chief among posttribulational arguments is the contention that anything else is new and novel, and that pretribulationalism in particular did not come into existence until about the year 1830. Although embodying the doubtful value of an "argument from silence," the charge is thought to be an unanswerable one and is pressed to the limit. Pretribulationalism has been variously attributed to the writings of Edward Irving, to the utterances of a woman-prophet in a trance, to the writings of Darby and his associates, to a godly clergyman named Tweedy, and ultimately to the Devil himself!

Some additional thoughts are found on page 223:

During these past nineteen centuries, there has been a progressive refinement of the details of Christian theology, but not until the last one hundred years has Eschatology come to the front to receive the major attention and scrutiny of foremost Bible scholars. It is not that the doctrine of Christ's coming, or any of its special features, is new or novel, but that the doctrine has finally come into the place of prominence it rightfully deserves.

Author Stanton then adds a further comment on page 226:

If God used Darby and his associates to restore to the Church doctrines long obscure and neglected, his name should be remembered with gratitude and not profaned as the originator of a twentieth century heresy. In this whole matter concerning the history of the imminent, pretribulational return of Jesus Christ, there is little by way of factual support or by way of attitudes taken to commend the writers from the posttribulational school.

One of the most popular books ever written upholding the pre-trib point of view is *The Rapture Question* (1957) by John F. Walvoord. He writes on page 15:

The third view, which is popular with premillenarians who have specialized in prophetic study, is the pretribulational position, which holds that Christ will come for His church before the entire seven-year period predicted by Daniel. The church in this point of view does not enter at all into the final tribulation period. This teaching was espoused by Darby and the Plymouth Brethren and popularized by the famous *Scofield Reference Bible*.

Later, on page 52, Walvoord again addresses the question of the two-stage origin:

One of the commonly repeated reasons for opposing pretribu-lationism is that it is a new and novel doctrine beginning no earlier than Darby. Reese, who is usually regarded as the outstanding champion of opponents of pretribulationism, states categorically that it is "a series of doctrines that had never been heard of before," that is, before the nineteenth century. Reese charges that the followers of Darby "sought to overthrow what, since the Apostolic Age, have been considered by all pre-millennialists as established results."
It must be conceded that the advanced and detailed theology of pretribulationism is not found in the Fathers, but neither is

any other detailed and "established" exposition of premillennialism. The development of most important doctrines took
centuries.

One of the largest volumes currently in circulation that
defends pre-tribulationism is *Things To Come* (1958) by J.
Dwight Pentecost. He touches briefly upon origins in three
places, starting at page 166:

> It was not until the last century that the field of Eschatology
> became a matter to which the mind of the church was turned.

On page 203 there appears a further comment:

> This doctrine of imminence, or "at any moment coming," is
> not a new doctrine with Darby, as is sometimes charged,
> although he did clarify, systematize, and popularize it.

And on page 391:

> The Biblical studies promoted by Darby and his followers
> popularized the premillennial interpretation of Scriptures.

The last book I'll take a look at is Hal Lindsey's popular
The Late Great Planet Earth (1970). Here is his statement on
page 181:

> Christians after the early second century spent little time
> really defining prophetic truth until the middle of the nineteenth
> century. Then there seems to have been a great revival of interest
> in the prophetic themes of the Bible.

There you have it—the answers given by leaders of the
pre-trib school of interpretation to charges made by post-
tribs that two-stage belief originated about 145 years ago in
Great Britain.

4. CAN A SCRIBE ASCRIBE?

So far, we've heard some post-trib charges and some pre-trib denials. But what do the historians say? Do they ascribe two-stage rapture principles to any definite source? Do the experts on origins know something the rest of us don't know?

The oldest book in this section is William B. Neatby's *A History of the Plymouth Brethren* (1901). On page 339 Neatby drew the following conclusion:

> Brethrenism is the child of the study of unfulfilled prophecy, and of the expectation of the immediate return of the Saviour. If any one had told the first Brethren that three quarters of a century might elapse and the Church be still on earth, the answer would probably have been a smile, partly of pity, partly of disapproval, wholly of incredulity. Yet so it has proved. It is impossible not to respect hopes so congenial to an ardent devotion; yet it is clear now that Brethrenism took shape under the influence of a delusion, and that that delusion was a decisive element in all its distinctive features.

Half a century later LeRoy E. Froom produced his massive work known as *The Prophetic Faith of Our Fathers* (1950), which included this insight on page 525 of Vol. III:

> . . . the "utterances" appeared, first in Scotland and then in London, in 1831, and were received as the gift of prophecy. During Irving's first tour of Scotland some young women had been healed by prayer. Later when supernatural manifestations began to appear, they claimed to have the gift of tongues. A favorable report from a delegation of Irving's congregation led

to the organization of meetings to seek the restoration of the
gifts.

Despair of the world's conversion by the ordinary methods of
evangelization, and the expectation of supernatural manifestations as a prelude to Christ's second advent, laid the foundation
for acceptance.

Harold H. Rowdon's *The Origins of the Brethren* (1967),
praised by Ernest R. Sandeen as "the best work in the field,"
contains this statement on page 16:

It was later alleged—and strenuously denied—that one of the
distinctive Brethren ideas regarding the Second Advent was of
Irvingite origin, and so we must briefly examine the Irvingite
background to the Brethren view that, prior to the open return of
Christ in judgement, He will return secretly in order to remove
His people from a doomed world.

As early as September, 1830, a distinction was drawn in an
article in *The Morning Watch* [an Irvingite journal] between the
'epiphany' and the 'advent' or 'parousia' of Christ. The former
was interpreted as His appearance in the sky which would strike
terror into the hearts of unbelievers and would be the signal for
the resurrection of dead saints and the changing of them and of
living saints in the act of rapture of I Thessalonians 4. 16, 17.
The advent, comprising the return of Christ and the saints to the
earth bringing judgement to the nations, was expected to follow.
The view that the saints would be caught up to heaven, like
Enoch and Elijah, was obviously a development of the idea that
they would be sheltered in some 'little sanctuary' from the
outpouring of divine judgement upon the earth.

On page 51 Rowdon throws some light on the formulation
of Darby's prophetic views:

A pamphlet which he published in 1829 reveals Darby's views
on the subject of prophecy at that time . . . . He held that the
prophecies of the return of the Jews to Palestine and their
restoration to the divine favour, which await fulfilment, implied
the apostasy and excision of the Gentile Church. This apostate
Church will not be confined to 'Popery', but will extend to 'the
dispensation of the Church generally'. At the same time, the

manifestation of Christ in judgement will make a suffering Church triumphant. This apparent paradox was not resolved, and indeed, Darby confessed that he had said nothing new. However, he expressed his willingness to return to the subject: nor did he fail to do so!

Rowdon continues on page 52 with still more information about Darby's progression in the realm of prophetic matters:

> Darby's next contribution to the study of unfulfilled prophecy was an article contributed to *The Christian Herald* [December, 1830, issue] and entitled 'On "Days" Signifying "Years" in Prophetic Language' . . . . The traditional view that Darby defended in the article was the idea that the periods of time denominated in the prophecies of Daniel and the Apocalypse in terms of months or years should be interpreted in terms of the day-year theory. He had not yet come to espouse the view, so important in his developed idea of the subject, that the fulfilment of the prophetic days was still future.

Another splendid work in the same area is *A History of the Brethren Movement* (1968), by F. Roy Coad. On page 63 Coad writes:

> Within a few weeks Bulteel was taken up violently by the rising craze for the "gifts" of healings and tongues so soon to be identified with the Irvingite movement. Wigram and Darby, at Newton's suggestion, had already investigated these "gifts" in the course of visits paid to their first place of occurrence at Row in Scotland, and had rejected them.

Coad then remarks on page 128:

> The tragedy of Bulteel at Oxford had sealed for Newton (if, indeed, it was not its cause) a violent antipathy to Irvingism, and with Irvingism everything that was connected with it. Notably, this rejection included a feature of prophetic interpretation which Darby had adopted, the doctrine of "the secret rapture of the saints."

On page 129 author Coad sheds further light in two paragraphs:

Into this [futurist] system both Darby and Irving had injected a further refinement, based upon a detailed attempt to reconcile the different parts of the New Testament which they considered to be relevant. In their view, the Second Advent would take place in two stages: first, there would be a quiet appearance—the "presence"—of Christ, when all true Christians, the true Church, would be removed from the earth. This was the "rapture of the saints." Only then, when the restraining presence of the Holy Spirit in His own people had been removed from the world scene, would Antichrist arise. His rule would be brought to an end by the second stage of the Advent—the public "appearing" of Christ in glory.

There was plainly a problem in this interpretation, and it was around this problem that the differences between Darby and Newton crystallized. If the Church were to be removed before the persecutions of Antichrist started, who then would be the faithful ones who would suffer at his hands? Newton's objection was a forcible one: if they were not of the Church, it was necessary to postulate another people of God, apart from the Church. Since, by his definition, the Church included all who were redeemed by Christ, this remnant must therefore be the fruits of a redemptive act of God other than the redemption through Christ. Thus, in Newton's view, the idea struck at the very heart of the orthodox doctrine of salvation, and was perilously near to postulating another Gospel and incurring the condemnation pronounced in Paul's letter to the Galatians.

Another recent work of great distinction is Ernest R. Sandeen's *The Roots of Fundamentalism* (1970). This author has much to say concerning the pre-trib rapture origin. Let's start with page 38:

> Darby used the third Powerscourt conference in September 1833 to continue his attack upon the apostasy of the churches and to stress the need for all true believers to gather in the name of the Lord alone. In a sense this was the first assembly of the new sect, but it was also the first occasion of disagreement between Darby and Newton. Darby introduced into discussion at Powerscourt the ideas of a secret rapture of the church and of a parenthesis in prophetic fulfillment between the sixty-ninth

and seventieth weeks of Daniel. These two concepts constituted the basic tenets of the system of theology since referred to as dispensationalism . . . . Neither Darby nor Newton seems to have become estranged at this time. Darby held an open mind on both of these subjects as late as 1843. Newton remembered, years later, opposing both positions. Commenting upon Darby's interpretation of the seventy weeks of Daniel, Newton remarked, "The secret rapture was bad enough, but this was worse."

Sandeen again refers to the secret rapture on pages 64–65:

Darby never indicated any source for his ideas other than the Bible—indeed, he consistently affirmed that his only theological task was explicating the text of Scripture. The secret rapture was a distinctive development, however, and considerable interest has been aroused about the source of the doctrine . . . . Darby's opponents claimed that the doctrine originated in one of the outbursts of tongues in Edward Irving's church about 1832. This seems to be a groundless and pernicious charge. Neither Irving nor any member of the Albury group advocated any doctrine resembling the secret rapture . . . . It is true that among the English phrases pronounced by one or another of the illuminati in Irving's church there occurred fragments such as "Behold the bridegroom cometh," and "count the days one thousand three score and two hundred—1,260— . . . at the end of which the saints of the Lord's should go up to meet the Lord in the air," but such utterances can scarcely be considered as evidence for any doctrine and have, in any case, little reference to the secret rapture as Darby taught it. Since the clear intention of this charge is to discredit the doctrine by attributing its origin to fanaticism rather than Scripture, there seems little ground for giving it any credence.

On page 90 Sandeen has two very interesting paragraphs:

The eschatological sections of Darby's theology seemed to exist as free elements in the religious atmosphere and were welcomed or banished according to criteria of verification that took no notice of the putative source. For whatever reason, the association of Darby with dispensationalism was not sufficient to destroy its attractiveness for non-Plymouth Brethren.

This line of reasoning raises a further question. Is it possible that one explanation for the disproportionate influence of this one aspect of Darby's theology upon other millenarians is that Darby was not alone in developing it? Is it possible that the doctrines of the secret rapture and parenthesis church were being taught simultaneously by several or even many prophetic students? If more were known about early nineteenth-century Irish Protestantism and, particularly, the intellectual history of Trinity College, Dublin, a clearer light might be thrown upon these puzzling and difficult points.

In this connection Sandeen adds a noteworthy comment in his bibliography section on page 289: "Relatively few manuscript collections have been discovered with direct relevance to this study."

The last book to be considered in this section is Iain H. Murray's *The Puritan Hope* (1971), another scholarly treatment touching upon two-stage developments. Page 200 exhibits Murray's thoughts:

All the salient features of Darby's scheme are to be found in Irving: the expectation of impending judgments upon Christendom, the imminence of Christ's advent, his consequent millennial reign upon earth—these beliefs, as we have already seen, were those of the Scottish preacher. There were, however, elaborations of detail. At Albury and in Irving's London congregation a curious belief, practically unknown in earlier Church history, had arisen, namely, that Christ's appearing before the millennium is to be in two stages, the first, a secret 'rapture' removing the Church before a 'Great Tribulation' smites the earth, the second his coming with his saints to set up his kingdom. This idea comes into full prominence in Darby. He held that 'the Church' is a mystery of which only Paul speaks. She is Christ's mystic body and will be complete at the 'rapture'. The Jews and other Gentiles converted thereafter will never be Christ's bride: 'I deny that saints before Christ's first coming, or after his second, are part of the Church.' With breath-taking dogmatism Darby swept away what had previously been axiomatic in Christian theology . . .

With reference to the above statement Murray says on page 286: "The link between Irving and Brethren prophetic beliefs seems to have been missed by most writers."

Many other historians have also referred to the beliefs arising in this period of English and Scottish history. But seemingly few have attempted to discover the exact origin of pre-tribulationism.

One could spend hours, for instance, in Margaret Oliphant's *The Life of Edward Irving* (1865) in search of some brief mention of a secret, two-stage rapture. She refers to "a new revelation" (page 290) which appeared in western Scotland in 1830, but fails to elaborate.

Edward Miller's two-volume set on *The History and Doctrines of Irvingism* (1878), though examining the development of the Irvingites, the Brethren, and even the Mormons, also has nothing on the origin of the two-stage coming.

The Catholic Apostolic Church (1946), by P. E. Shaw, likewise is unaware of any pre-trib rapture origin; the author has a chapter on "The Charismatic Period" and includes portions of one of Margaret Macdonald's revelations, but it lacks even an allusion to the origin of two-stage tenets.

Although B. B. Warfield's *Miracles: Yesterday and Today* (1953) contains 27 pages on the Irvingite gifts, there are only two or three references to Margaret Macdonald's healing and not a word about any two-stage revelation.

Fascination with the Catholic Apostolic Church and related topics continues today.

Larry Christenson, in *A Message to the Charismatic Movement* (1972), acknowledges the charismatic manifestations in Scotland and England in the early part of the last century and relates them to glossalalia of the present time. But he does not seek to uncover the start of pre-tribulationism, even though he does make mention of the healing of Margaret Macdonald and Mary Campbell.

Having examined what the historians have (and have not) said, we are compelled to ask if it is possible that some unknown person was the *real* originator of the two-stage rapture?

Maybe a long, hard look at the early 1800s will turn up something. Let's see what was going on then.

5. NARROWING THE NINETEENTH

When the nineteenth century rolled around, most folks had little inkling of what was to take place within a few years. That is, in the field of biblical prophecy.

During the Protestant Reformation many, if not most, of the reformers believed that the Roman papacy was the Antichrist. They thought that the prophecies of the book of Revelation would not be fulfilled in the future, but that the fulfillment had been taking place all throughout the church age.

In other words, they followed the "historic" (historicist) or "Protestant" method of interpretation, as contrasted with the "futurist" type of interpretation which sees prophetic portions of Scripture ahead of us in the future and still waiting to be fulfilled.

Some of the persons in this "historic" school of thinking were pre-mill in outlook, but most were a-mill.

Then in the 1700s another system of interpretation known as post-millennialism captured many minds. An early leader of this post-mill movement, which continued many years and then largely collapsed after the recent world wars, was Daniel Whitby (1638–1726). He thought the world would get better and better and that the Church would usher in the millennium before Christ's second advent. The "historic" interpretation could also be found in post-mill circles.

One of the features of this "historic" approach was the belief that the 1260 days in the period of tribulation were actually 1260 years. This was called the year-day theory, belief in which often led to the setting of dates for the Lord's return.

Prophetic writers, calculating the dates to be found in the book of Daniel, usually determined that the tribulation started with the edict of Justinian in A.D. 533. The French Revolution of 1793 came 1260 years after that date and not a few persons thought that Napoleon was the Antichrist. When the nineteenth century finally arrived there was talk that the year 1823 would be one of special significance, since it would occur 1290 years after the Justinian edict.

Early in the 1800s a strong reaction to post-millennialism set in, in the form of a movement which greatly emphasized the return of Christ. We would call it a prophetic revival! British newspapers and journals gave a lot of space to the discussion of prophecy, Bible conferences stressing prophetic subjects soon appeared, and the imminent return of Christ was the topic of the day.

The year-day theory was still popular with many folk, but began to lose followers after events failed to transpire at the predicted times. It was gradually replaced with what became known as the "futurist" interpretation. Futurists of the first three decades of the last century held that Antichrist would be a world ruler at the end of the age who would persecute all true Christians during the great tribulation.

One of the earliest and most important prophetic conferences was held annually from 1826–1830 at Albury Manor. This was banker Henry Drummond's palatial home (still standing today) located in a beautiful rural setting about thirty miles southwest of London, England.[1] Other important prophetic meetings of that era were convened, after the Albury conferences, in Lady Theodosia Powerscourt's mansion about fifteen miles south of Dublin, Ireland. (Powerscourt House was gutted by fire in November of 1974.)

For a century and a half historians have associated two men—Edward Irving and John Darby—with these early conferences and with the futurist development of this period.

* * *

Edward Irving was born on August 4, 1792, in Annan, Scotland. He entered Edinburgh University when he was thirteen years old and received an M.A. in April, 1809, when he was only sixteen. He was licensed a Presbyterian minister in June of 1815 and four years later was the assistant to Dr. Thomas Chalmers in his parish in Glasgow. In 1822 Irving became pastor of the Caledonian Chapel (Presbyterian) at Hatton Garden in London. His fame as a great orator soon spread throughout the entire area.

Irving was born when post-millennialism was still exerting a strong influence. The early 1800s saw a revival of pre-millennialism which was "historic" in outlook, that is, holding that the papacy was the Antichrist and viewing the 1260 days as 1260 years. Irving was influenced for a time by this type of pre-millennialism, a leader of which was J. H. Frere.

But futurist pre-millennialism was also on the scene. Irving discovered Manuel de Lacunza's *The Coming of Messiah in Glory and Majesty* (1812) and in 1826 translated this Spanish book into English. Lacunza, who wrote the book under the pen name of Juan Josafat Ben-Ezra, saw a future Antichrist which would not be an individual but rather a corrupted Roman Catholic priesthood. At least one writer has suggested that this book originated the pre-trib rapture theory, but a close examination of it rules out any such conclusion.[2] The year 1826 also marked the first of the Albury prophetic conferences. Irving was an important figure at these annual meetings.

In the meantime Irving's London congregation had grown to such an extent that a new church was built near the southwest corner of Regent Square and opened on May 11, 1827.[3]

As early as 1828 Irving had decided that the spiritual gifts of the apostolic age really belonged to the church of all ages, and that they had largely disappeared because of a lack of faith. A prolific writer of books and pamphlets, he promulgated his views upholding the apostolic gifts and the return of Christ, which he said was not only imminent but would be preceded by an end-time outpouring of such gifts. The titles of some of his writings at this time were: *On the Restoration of Spiritual Gifts* (1828), *The Last Days: their character evil* (1828), *Book of Revelation interpreted* (1829), and *Daniel's vision of the Four Beasts* (1829).

Irving, who has been called "the father of modern Pentecostalism," could hardly have been shocked when news reached him in the middle of 1830 that a charismatic revival had broken out in some towns in western Scotland.

Among the many who went up from England in person to investigate the phenomenon was a delegation from Irving's own church. And the last Albury conference, meeting in July of 1830, upon hearing of the Scottish manifestations passed a resolution to inquire into them. Excitement filled the air!

The Morning Watch, an Irvingite prophetic journal of the times, published an article in September of 1830 which drew a distinction between the *epiphany* and the *parousia*, the first term being the first stage of the Lord's second coming and the second term pointing to the second stage.[4] Since then the Irvingites (better known as the Catholic Apostolic Church) have continued to teach a split rapture which includes a pre-trib first stage.[5]

Throughout the autumn of 1830 prayer meetings to seek a similar outpouring of the Holy Spirit were held in private homes in London. One such meeting was held in the house of J. B. Cardale, leader of the Albury delegation to Scotland. The first known case of speaking in tongues in London was experienced by Cardale's wife on April 30, 1831, when she also uttered the following prophecy: "The Lord will speak to His people—the Lord hasteneth His Coming—the Lord cometh." A short time later the Cardales joined Irving's church.[6] The tongues and related prophesyings were soon heard regularly in the Regent Square church and became the talk of all London, including the newspapers and Irving's unsympathetic denominational officials. Finally the Trustees of the church filed a complaint against Irving with the Presbytery of London. Trial was held by the Presbytery in the church on April 26, 1832. Irving was found guilty of violating Presbyterian order by allowing the services to be interrupted with unauthorized utterances (tongues and prophecy) and was ordered to be removed from his church. On Sunday morning, May 6, the Trustees locked Irving and his followers (most of the congregation) out of the building. They began to meet instead in a building in Gray's Inn Road. It was there that the Catholic Apostolic Church was born.

Ironically, Irving himself never spoke in tongues or prophesied, and he was finally deposed from the ministry altogether by his hometown presbytery of Annan on charges of Christological heresy (he taught that when Christ became incarnate he fully assumed sinful human nature so that his sinless life depended on the power of the Holy Spirit, not on an innately sinless human nature).[7] That trial took place March 13, 1833. His subsequent leadership in the Catholic Apostolic Church was short-lived. He died on December 7, 1834, and was buried in a crypt in Glasgow Cathedral. He had lived only forty-two years.

John Nelson Darby was born on November 18, 1800, in London, England. He entered Trinity College in Dublin, Ireland, in 1815 when he was fourteen and graduated four years later.

Although he studied law, Darby apparently never practiced law to any great extent, turning instead to a life of spiritual endeavors. An Anglican, he became a deacon in 1825. The following year he was ordained a priest. He served in that capacity for a time in County Wicklow, directly south of Dublin. Soon Darby and some of his friends began to conduct home worship services; from these informal gatherings the Brethren movement grew.[8]

The year 1827 witnessed an accident which changed Darby's life; a horse threw him against a doorpost and during the length of convalescence he had plenty of time to meditate upon the Bible. During this period Darby began formulating his dispensational ideas. Ernest Sandeen says Darby apparently felt in later years that he had been convinced of the secret rapture doctrine during this time. But a careful search of Darby's writings does not back up Sandeen's assertion.[9]

Darby, like Irving, had been born at a time when the post-mill view was quite influential. Both men later came under the sway of the historic pre-mill school with its year-day program. And both eventually switched to the futurist pre-mill point of view with its future Antichrist.

The Collected Writings of J. N. Darby, edited by William Kelly, contain four prophetic volumes. The first item in Prophetic Vol. 1, covering thirty-one pages, is a pamphlet which Darby originally published in Dublin in 1829.[10] In it there is no mention of a secret, pre-trib rapture. He sees, instead, a suffering church on earth until the coming of Christ in judgment. Here is a portion of the pamphlet:

> "They answered and said unto him, Where, Lord? And he said unto them, Wheresoever the body is, thither will the eagles be gathered together." If these things be so, there will be a direct manifestation of Christ, of the judicial power of the Lamb, quite distinct from any of the present expectations of those who reject the study of prophecy. When John saw heaven opened and beheld a white horse, and He that sat upon him called Faithful and True, and in righteousness doth He judge and make war—when he saw the Person and glory of the Word of God, it was the revelation of something wholly different from the secret operations of the Spirit of God; and it was something characteristically different from previous providential judgments. These had been hail, and thunder, and lightning, and earthquakes; but this was a manifestation of Him who had been long hid behind instruments, who had governed the world as one that apparently suffered His church to grow up and spring He knew not how, because the harvest of the earth was ripe. The ordained government of the earth and the operation of the Spirit of God was that by which He has ruled the church hitherto; therefore it was a suffering church. Now He was Himself manifested in His power, and therefore the church became triumphant.[11]

Darby admits at the end of this pamphlet that his prophetic views have not changed drastically. He says: "The writer, believing that in the rapid accumulation of inquiry he could add but little new to the investigation of this subject, has refrained from trespassing upon others." [12] Later in the same paragraph (and still talking about the subject of prophecy) he promises his readers that "if occasion seem to call, he will, with gladness, resume the subject, in communion with the church." [13] Little did Darby realize at that time how soon, and in what manner, he would resume the subject!

In December of 1830 an article by Darby was included in *The Christian Herald*, a prophetic journal published in Dublin. The title: "On 'Days' Signifying 'Years' in Prophetic Language." The article was a defense of the historic pre-mill view of the year-day theory. (The *historical* pre-mill view, as outlined by Reese in the second chapter of this book, is not the same as the historic, year-day view.) Darby's futurist pre-trib rapture idea was still yet to come.

Brethren writer William Kelly, in a twenty-three-page pamphlet which came out in 1903, said Darby confessed in 1850 that he had discovered in 1830, by studying II Thessalonians 2:1–2, that the Rapture would precede the Day of the Lord. Kelly also told of a letter from Darby to Benjamin Newton, another early Brethren member, in which Darby revealed that a Mr. T. Tweedy, a member of the Brethren in Ireland, apparently had cleared up the exegetical difficulties Darby had at first encountered with that text.[14]

Darby's article, since it appeared in December, 1830, and yet made no mention of this discovery, may seem to present a problem in timing. If, however, we determine that Darby wrote the article several months, or even several weeks, before the December issue in which it appeared, then it isn't unreasonable to conclude that Darby became convinced of pre-trib rapturism after he had written and submitted the article.

Brethren historian Harold Rowdon, says that, according to Newton, the Brethren in Plymouth were clearly teaching a two-stage coming as early as the second Sunday that the Plymouth chapel was being used, which dates it no later than 1831.[15] The pre-trib rapture continued to undergo development among the Brethren in Ireland and was discussed at great length at the annual Powerscourt prophetic conferences. These meetings started in 1831 and continued several years. Sandeen says it was Darby who introduced the topic of a secret rapture at the 1833 Powerscourt session.[16]

Dissension on the rapture issue raged for many years in Brethren circles, two main antagonists being Darby and Newton. Sandeen adds that Darby still entertained doubts about his secret rapture belief as late as 1843 or 1845.[17]

The two-stage coming view of the Brethren spread to America and other parts of the world in the latter part of the century. Darby visited the U.S. at least five times. His dispensationalism became part of the *Scofield Reference Bible* (1909). Darby died on April 29, 1882, at 81 years of age.

Some writers have suggested that Victorinus, who lived in the third century, hinted at a secret rapture, but it is relatively certain that no body of Christians ever taught it before the 1830s.[18] Significantly, neither Darby nor Irving ever claimed to have originated a secret pre-trib rapture. Both, however, definitely taught it. The Irvingites were teaching it, as we have already noted, as early as September of 1830 in their prophetic journal *The Morning Watch*. And I think we can conclude that Darby was attempting to verify it by Scripture towards the end of 1830. We also know that the Brethren in Plymouth, England, took up this teaching not long after that.

Is it possible that some little-known person was teaching two-stage or pre-trib doctrine before Irving and Darby taught it?

And if so, did any such person ever claim to have originated it?

Were such beliefs ever committed to writing and put into circulation before Irving and Darby took up similar views?

Did both Irving and Darby know any such individual before they began teaching a pre-trib rapture?

Believe it or not, the answer to all of these questions is *Yes!*

NOTES

1. Drummond's many-chimneyed mansion is today an apartment complex for elderly retired persons. On November 24, 1972, my wife and I were graciously allowed to tour the inside including the massive library where prophetic sessions were held. Drummond is buried nearby in a 900-year-old Saxon chapel.

2. Duncan McDougall in *The Rapture of the Saints*, pp. 15, 31 (*Old Fashioned Prophecy Magazine* revised edition, 1970). Lacunza's notion that the shout, voice of the archangel, and trump of God will occur "much before His arrival at earth" hardly resembles two-stage rapturism, especially since he tied in these I Thessalonians 4 aspects with the time "when the Lord returns from heaven to earth." Moreover, Lacunza believed that the Church will be on earth until the time of the judgments accompanying the return of Christ in glory to set up His kingdom.

3. Irving's National Scotch Church on Regent Square in London was bombed during World War II. Today a Reformed Church stands on the same site.

4. Referring to this article entitled "On the Epiphany of our Lord Jesus Christ and the Gathering of His Elect," Rowdon's *The Origins of the Brethren* (1967), pp. 30–31, points out that, interestingly enough, later Brethren writers completely reversed these terms; to them the *parousia* was the rapture and the *epiphany* Christ's return to earth. One might ask: are there really two stages to the Lord's return if such terms are so evidently interchangeable?

5. Their split rapture is actually a series of raptures. Robert Norton's *The Restoration of Apostles and Prophets; In the Catholic Apostolic Church* (1861), p. 171, reveals that church's doctrine to the effect "that these are the last days; that the Lord is now coming again; that before revealing Himself to the world as its Judge, He will reveal Himself to His church as her glorious Bridegroom: and not to all at once; but first of all to His sealed ones, as the first fruits of a general harvest, of which they shall be the angel-reapers." Norton (1807–1883) was one of the chief chroniclers of the C. A. C.

6. Mrs. John B. Cardale uttered this in a home prayer meeting before joining Irving's group. She is probably the woman some writers have

in mind when they speak of "a woman's utterance in Irving's church." After the Cardale family became members of Irving's church, both she and her husband's sister, Emily, were among the leading prophetesses there.

7. For a thorough discussion of this question see *The Pentecostal Theology of Edward Irving* by Gordon Strachan (1973).

8. The term "Plymouth Brethren" originally designated the Brethren who met for worship in Plymouth, England. Mostly outsiders have applied this name to the Brethren as a whole.

9. Ernest R. Sandeen, *The Roots of Fundamentalism* (1970), p. 64. In only one of two passages cited for support is the year 1827 mentioned and in this 1863 letter (*Letters of J.N.D.*, reprint 1971, Vol. 1, p. 344) Darby follows the reference to 1827 by saying: "the house character of the assembly on earth (not the fact of the presence of the Spirit) was subsequently. It was a vague fact which received form in my mind long after, that there must be a wholly new order of things . . . ." Sandeen's other means of support is a letter dated only 185_ (*Letters of J.N.D.*, reprint 1971, Vol. 3, p. 299) in which Darby, looking back to the period in question, speaks of his early discovery of distinctions between Israel and the church, and then adds: "I was not able to put these things in their respective places or arrange them in order, as I can now . . . ." In neither of these two letters does Darby mention belief in a pre-trib rapture; he adopted that later.

10. Entitled *Reflections Upon the Prophetic Inquiry and the Views Advanced in it.*

11. *The Collected Writings of J. N. Darby* (reprint 1971), Prophetic Volume No. 1, pp. 28–29.

12. *Ibid.*, pp. 30–31.

13. *Ibid.*, p. 31.

14. W. Kelly, *The Rapture of the Saints: Who Suggested it, or Rather on What Scripture?* (1903), pp. 5–6. Rowdon's *The Origins of the Brethren* (1967), p. 97, says Newton later thought that Darby's letter to him concerning Tweedy had been written either in 1832 or 1833.

15. Harold H. Rowdon, *The Origins of the Brethren* (1967), p. 82. On the same page, in a footnote, Rowdon adds that Newton and Tregelles dated the initial service at Plymouth in 1831, but that D. J. Beattie's *Brethren* (1940), pp. 18–19, dated it 1830.

16. Sandeen, *op. cit.*, p. 38.

17. *Ibid.*, p. 64.

18. LeRoy E. Froom's *The Prophetic Faith of Our Fathers* (1950), Vol. I, p. 340, speaks of Victorinus' "strange interpretation" of Apocalyptic events: for instance, the moon as blood referring to persecution, and the heaven rolled away interpreted as the church being taken away. Froom adds that Victorinus also saw (in the mountains and islands removed out of their places) the good persons being removed to avoid

coming persecution. Victorinus' actual words, however, as translated by Alexander Roberts and James Donaldson in *The Ante-Nicene Fathers* (1886), Vol. VII, p. 351, are these: "Mountains and islands removed from their places intimate that in the last persecution all men departed from their places; that is, that the good will be removed, seeking to avoid the persecution." All I see in Victorinus' statement is the scene of men fleeing *in time of persecution;* they "departed" because they were "seeking," and ended up in a state of being "removed." Moreover, Victorinus said later in the same discourse (*Commentary on the Apocalypse of the Blessed John*) that he viewed the sun-clothed woman of Revelation 12, who is preserved in the wilderness during the tribulation, as a symbol of the church.

6. NORTON THE NARRATOR

In the summer of 1971 I was haunted by a certain question: who was the woman in Edward Irving's church who made that utterance some writers refer to, and what did she really say? A few books state that pre-trib rapture teaching began as a result of one woman's charismatic utterance, and it wasn't long before my journalistic curiosity was thoroughly aroused. I determined to search until I had found the answers—no matter how long it took.

In the days that followed I came across two books by American authors which contain material on the pre-trib origin.[1] Both writers had been influenced by John A. Anderson, M.D., of Aberdeen, Scotland, and his book entitled *Heralds of the Dawn* (1946).[2]

Anderson maintains in his book on page 40 that a Miss M. M. had originated the two-stage coming theory in March of 1830 in Great Britain. He based this assertion on an old book called *The Restoration of Apostles and Prophets; In the Catholic Apostolic Church*, written under the initials R. N. which, according to Anderson (and the American authors), belonged to a Dr. R. Nolan. But I soon discovered that the catalogues of the British Museum and Library of Congress, and other reference sources, had no listing of any Nolan who had authored such a book.

Later that same summer I read in Edward Miller's *The History and Doctrines of Irvingism* (1878), that R. N. was really R. Norton (not R. Nolan). The British Museum catalogue showed that R. Norton was Rev. Robert Norton, M.D., a British clergyman who wrote the book in 1861.

During that time one scholar in Pennsylvania told me he had searched for Norton's book all his life without success. At about the same time a professor in California who was a rare book collector asked me to notify him if I should find a copy.[3] On October 20, 1971, while rummaging through stacks of uncatalogued and not-for-sale books on Irvingism in the back of an Illinois bookstore, I discovered a rare copy of Norton's book and persuaded the owner to sell it to me.[4]

Miss M. M., according to Norton's first chapter, was Margaret Macdonald of Port Glasgow, Scotland.[5] Excitedly thumbing through the pages, I soon found what I was looking for:

> Marvellous light was shed upon Scripture, and especially on the doctrine of the second Advent, by the revived spirit of prophecy. In the following account by Miss M. M—, of an evening during which the power of the Holy Ghost rested upon her for several successive hours, in mingled prophecy and vision, we have an instance; for here we first see the distinction between that final stage of the Lord's coming, when every eye shall see Him, and His prior appearing in glory to them that look for Him.[6]

There are two astonishing admissions in this paragraph. Norton says Margaret Macdonald saw a two-stage coming, and that this was the *first* time such a distinction was made! Immediately after this amazing paragraph are these words:

> She writes:—"I felt this needed to be revealed, and that there was great darkness and error about it; but suddenly what it was burst upon me with a glorious light.[7]

And then, without interruption, Margaret's statement continues on the next three pages and ends at the bottom of page 18.[8]

Norton is probably the only person who ever preserved Margaret Macdonald's pre-trib revelation in a book. Actu-

ally, he included it in two books. He first published it in his
Memoirs of James & George Macdonald, of Port-Glasgow
(1840), pages 171–176, and immediately prefaced her statement by writing: "The following paper being recollections of
a certain evening, having already, though surreptitiously, got
into circulation, has been so much identified with the work of
the Spirit in the two brothers, that it seems right to insert it
here."

But just how reliable is Norton as a writer? Did he get his
information directly from Margaret, or was it second-hand
material? What are the available facts about him?

He was born in the Bermondsey district of South London
on Saturday, September 19, 1807. The handwritten birth
certificate reads:

> On the Nineteenth Day of the Ninth Month one thousand
> eight hundred and seven was born in Grange Road in the Parish
> called St. Mary Magdalen Bermondsey in the County of Surrey
> unto Thomas Norton of Grange Road Wheelwright and Eliza-
> beth his wife a Son who was named Robert.[9]

Desiring to become a medical doctor, Norton studied at
Edinburgh University's Faculty of Medicine from 1826 to
1829. Interestingly, Charles Darwin was also a student there
from 1825 to 1827, so that Norton's first year coincided with
his last year.

On the 1826 matriculation sheet, which listed 233 students,
Norton's home address was still in London. His signature,
appearing on this sheet, was much the same as in later years.
He graduated in 1829, when he was only twenty-one and
received his M.D. His doctoral thesis, written in Latin, was
entitled: "De Fabricae origanicae Vitiis a quibus pendet
Dyspepsia." A rough English translation: "Concerning the
faults of the hereditary structure on which indigestion
depends."

When news of the charismatic revival in western Scotland,
which included reports of miraculous healing, reached London and other cities in the late spring of 1830, Norton, a

devout Anglican as well as a doctor, went there as an observer along with many others. (John Darby of the Brethren was another one who journeyed to Scotland to see things for himself. We'll discuss his findings later on.)

Norton later reported his observations from that trip in his first book, which was published in 1839 while he resided at Hillhead in Greenock, Scotland, a town only a few miles west of Port Glasgow.[10] He wrote:

> On the other hand, the opposite class of characteristics, the scriptural and the heavenly, I fear not to say, have been *as manifestly* the characteristics of those prophetic manifestations which I here advocate, and respecting which I cannot but bear my humble, yet most solemn testimony, that the daily and hourly observation of successive years, has only confirmed my original conviction that they have been of God. Feelings of personal delicacy, and of doubt respecting its propriety, alone prevent me from occupying pages, with notes and recollections of utterances, each one of which would show how purely scriptural, how spiritual, how glorifying to Jesus, their character has been . . . .[11]
>
> The two principal brethren [James and George Macdonald] whose mouths were then opened to confess and glorify their Lord, are now with him whom their souls loved; and I can scarcely refrain from transcribing, from the notes of that day a few sentences of one of their many songs of rapturous adoration. Alas! that so little else than a few imperfect recollections, should now remain of either of them; for there was about them both, at times, when the power of the Spirit was most upon them, such heavenliness and awe-inspiring solemnity in their whole appearance and manner; such deep-toned inimitable music in their voices; such ecstatic rapture in their eye; yea, (for I cannot but speak the things which I have seen and heard,) such a supernatural brightness upon their countenances, as stamped upon their utterances a seal of divinity, the impression of which is quite incommunicable.[12]

The next year Norton, still living in Greenock, produced the *Memoirs of James & George Macdonald.*

The call to the ministry soon pushed aside the previous call to medicine and, in the early 1840s Dr. Norton enrolled as a student at the Clerical College in St. Bees, which today is a small resort town on the western coast of England in the northern county of Cumberland.

On Sunday, November 24, 1844, a public notice of Norton's intention to declare himself a candidate for the office of deacon in the Church of England was read aloud during a worship service in the St. Bees parish church. The two-page, handwritten notice, signed by the officiating minister and two other persons, reads as follows:

> Notice is hereby given that Robert Norton M.D.—now student of the clerical college of St. Bees, and resident in this parish, intends to offer himself a candidate for the holy office of a deacon, at the ensuing ordination of the Lord Bishop of Ripon; and if any person knows any just cause or impediment, for which he ought not to be admitted into holy orders, he is now to declare the same, or to signify the same forthwith to the Lord Bishop of Ripon.
>
> We do hereby certify that the above notice was publicly read by the undersigned T. C. Grier in the parish church of St. Bees in the county of Cumberland, during the time of divine service, on Sunday the 24th day of November in the year of our Lord one thousand eight hundred and forty four.

Three days after this public notice was read in church, a letter stating Norton's intentions of becoming an Anglican deacon was sent to The Right Reverend Charles Thomas, the Lord Bishop of Ripon. The letter, signed by the principal of the Clerical College of St. Bees and one of the theological lecturers, reads:

> To The Right Reverend the Lord Bishop of Ripon.
> Whereas our well beloved in Christ Robert Norton hath declared to us his intention of offering himself a candidate for the sacred office of a deacon, & for that end hath requested of us letters testimonial of his learning & good behaviour; we therefore, whose names are hereunto subscribed, do testify that the

said Robert Norton having been previously known to us for the space of nearly two years (wanting only one month) last past, hath during that time lived piously, soberly, & honestly, & diligently applied himself to his studies; nor hath he at any time so far as we know & believe, held, written, or taught any thing contrary to the doctrine or discipline of the united church of England & Ireland; and moreover, we believe him in our consciences to be a person worthy to be admitted to the sacred order of deacon. In witness whereof we have subscribed our names this 27th day of the month of November in the year of our Lord one thousand eight hundred & forty four.

On the ninth of January following Norton wrote to T. Burder Esq. regarding his forthcoming appointment as curate in the Church at Rothwell:

> Denison Hall, Hanover Square
> Leeds
> Sir, I herewith forward my testimonials & other papers. You will notice two peculiarities about them which it is perhaps necessary for me to explain. The first is that I have sent my only legal & attainable proof of my age—in the shape of a Quaker certificate of birth, having been born in their community & only of late years baptized.
> The second is that my testimonials extend only to the last two years instead of the usual period (three).
> This however is with the Bishop's knowledge, consent, as it arises simply from my having been out of England & travelling about during the preceding year.

A letter dated the next day, January 10, written by the Reverend John Bele, vicar of the church in Rothwell (near Leeds), to the Bishop of Ripon, on the appointment of Norton as curate (assistant minister) in the Rothwell church, follows:

> These are to certify that I John Bele A.M. Vicar of Rothwell, in the County of York, and your Lordships Diocese of Ripon, do hereby nominate and appoint Robert Norton, of St. Bees Coll., to perform the office of a Curate in my Church, and do promise

to allow him the yearly sum of twenty-five pounds for his maintenance in the same, and to continue him to officiate as Curate in my said Church, until he shall be provided with some Ecclesiastical preferment, unless for any fault of his committed he shall be lawfully removed from the same. And I hereby do solemnly declare that I do not fraudulently give this certificate to entitle the said Robert Norton to receive Holy Orders, but with a real intention, to employ him in my said Church, according to what is before expressed.

The next year, 1846, Norton became curate of St. Matthew's Church (still standing) in Holbeck, another city in the Leeds area, and remained there until 1854. His signature appears on numerous marriage certificates, still extant in the Leeds Archives Library.[13]

Since his trip to Scotland in 1830 Norton had become increasingly convinced that he was living in the last days and that before Christ was to return for His church there would be a restoration of apostles and prophets. Much of this thinking began to crystallize during his service at St. Matthew's, as a list of the pamphlets he wrote in those years will show: *The Antitype of the Passover in the Worship of Christian Families* (1852); *The Nearness of the Second Coming of Christ* (1852); *Reasons for Believing that the Lord has Restored to the Church Apostles and Prophets* (1852); *A Discourse on the Faith and Hope of the Catholic Apostolic Church* (1854); and *The Restoration of Apostles and Prophets in the Catholic Apostolic Church* (1854). The last pamphlet was originally a letter to the Bishop of Ripon, not the 191-page book by the same title which came out in 1861.[14] In that 1854 letter to the Bishop he spoke of his intention to resign from the Church of England (which he carried out soon thereafter). Part of his letter reads:

. . . one object of this Letter is to vindicate from misapprehension, my purposed Resignation of my present Parochial Charge; principally because the burthen of it, is too great for me without the entire sympathy and support of my Bishop; although with it, I could gladly still proclaim within the Church of England that fulness of truth, which at present she has not; and in the wilful want of which, persisting until the end, how hopeless will her state be! I therefore repeat, that the rebuilding of the Catholic Apostolic Church, is not in antagonism to other Christian communities, but is a Centre for their union;—neither does communion with the Apostles through the laying on of their hands, without which none can be among the 144,000 sealed ones, who shall escape the impending tribulation under the reign of Antichrist—require that any unless specially called or circumstanced, should abandon any station of life or sphere of duty, so long as they can serve God faithfully and effectually in it.

From 1857 to 1862 Norton lived at Albury in southern England, a village famous for prophetic conferences several decades earlier. There he was engaged in the service of the Albury Catholic Apostolic Church which Henry Drummond had built not far from his mansion.[15] In 1861 he published *The Restoration of Apostles and Prophets; In the Catholic Apostolic Church.*

From 1862 until his death in 1883 Norton lived in London. His writings during this last stretch of earthly days included: *The True Position and Hope of the Catholic Apostolic Church* (1866); *Agnus Dei: The Lamb of God* (1867); *Truths and Untruths; Respecting a Restored Apostolate* (1876); and *Primary Truths of Christianity: for "The Hour of Temptation"* (1878).

His last residence was 32 St. Mary's Terrace in the Paddington district of west London.[16] On the 31st of January, 1883, this almost unknown and unsung chronicler of the pre-trib rapture origin, died at seventy-five years of age.[17]

In this chapter we've briefly gone over the life and writings of Robert Norton. Now it's time to return to the 1830 charismatic revival in western Scotland and find out more about Miss Margaret Macdonald.

NOTES

1. Moreton F. Scruby, *Immediately After the Tribulation* (1951), and Wesley G. Edwards, *The Day of Vengeance* (circa 1964).
2. The foreword of which was written by Henry W. Frost, then the Director-Emeritus of the China Inland Mission.
3. Norman F. Douty and Wilbur M. Smith, respectively.
4. At the present time I know of only eight copies of this book in the entire world; while researching in London in late 1972 I also purchased the only copy that could be found in the Catholic Apostolic Church Library in Gordon Square, where outsiders have lately been permitted to browse and buy certain works.
5. After discovering Norton's rare volume in a Naperville, Illinois, bookstore in the fall of 1971, my wife and I had lunch a short distance away at (you guessed it) a McDonald's drive-in restaurant!
6. R. N., [Robert Norton, M.D.] *The Restoration of Apostles and Prophets; In the Catholic Apostolic Church* (1861), p. 15.
7. Scruby's book also includes this sentence, but Edwards and Anderson quote none of Margaret's words in their books.
8. Margaret's several-page revelatory statement, as it appears in a slightly longer form in Norton's *Memoirs of James & George Macdonald, of Port-Glasgow* (1840), pp. 171–176, is included at the back of this book as an appendix. Oliphant includes a June 2, 1830, letter written by Edward Irving in *The Life of Edward Irving* (1865), pp. 292–293, which shows how early and to what extent Margaret's writings were being circulated; Irving writes: "The substance of Mary Campbell's and Margaret Macdonald's visions or revelations, given in their papers, carry to me a spiritual conviction and a spiritual reproof which I cannot express." Margaret's original handwritten statement of her pre-trib revelation could very well be among certain inaccessible papers stored today at the Catholic Apostolic Church Library in London's Gordon square.
9. I am extremely grateful to British scholar Jack Green of Hemsworth, Yorkshire, for his valuable assistance in obtaining photocopies of this and other early Norton documents at the Archives Library in Leeds, England, several of which are included in this chapter.
10. The long title: *Neglected and Controverted Scripture Truths; With an Historical Review of Miraculous Manifestations in the Church of Christ; and an Account of their Late Revival in the West of Scotland.* The author's name on the title page is given as Robert Norton, M.D., although in later years some of his works carried R. Norton, or just R. N. His last writings often gave the simple by-line—By a Clergyman.

11. *Ibid.,* p. 395.
12. *Ibid.,* p. 396. P. E. Shaw's *The Catholic Apostolic Church* (1946), p. 33, also says Norton was an eyewitness of these occurrences in Scotland in 1830. See also Norton's *Restoration* (1861), p. 38.
13. There seems to be complete silence as to whether or not Norton was ever married.
14. Phrases and quotes written in French, Greek, and Latin can be found in Norton's writings. A. L. Drummond's *Edward Irving and His Circle* [1937], p. 147, speaks of Norton's excellent educational background.
15. Also known as the Apostles' Chapel. On Friday, November 24, 1972, the caretaker graciously unlocked the back door and took us on a tour inside the sanctuary which, he related, last saw services in the early 1950s. The church is a five-minute walk from Albury Manor.
16. This street address was an apartment in the Park Place Villas, all of which were destroyed by bombs in World War II.
17. I own a certified copy of Norton's death certificate which I obtained at London's Somerset House (birth, marriage, and death records); the listed causes of death were senility, heart failure, and atony of bladder and intestinal canal. The certificate lists his occupation at the time of death as a clerk in holy orders.

7. PATTERN OF EVENTS

Many writers drawing attention to the 1830 Scottish revival of charismatic gifts seem to know little about its traceable beginnings and underlying causes. Earlier in the nineteenth century, as we have seen, there had been an increase of interest in the futurist school of prophetic interpretation. Many people were drawn to examine afresh the Bible's prophecies concerning the end of the world. In addition societies had been formed for the conversion of the Jews, for educating the lower classes, for taking the gospel to the heathen, and for distributing the Scriptures around the world.

Robert Norton's *The Restoration of Apostles and Prophets; In the Catholic Apostolic Church* throws much valuable light on the years immediately preceding the 1830 charismatic outburst, as does another little-known work touching on this period, *Supplementary Narrative to the Elijah Ministry* (1868) by C. W. Boase.[1] Reading them, one learns that, during those years, certain pious individuals in Great Britain began noticing the promises of Scripture having to do with "the latter rain" and related topics.[2] In 1826 James Haldane Stewart, a Church of England clergyman, suggested that churches all across the land schedule weekly prayer meetings for the outpouring of the Holy Spirit.[3]

Things soon began to happen on both the north and south banks of the Clyde River in western Scotland. There the Rev. John McLeod Campbell preached in the town of Row on the north bank of the river.[4] Although the Scotch (Presbyterian) Church at that time strongly upheld the doctrine that Christ had died only for the elect, Campbell preached the universal love of God and declared that all could be saved by the blood of Christ and that Christ died for all.[5] According to Boase, people came from considerable distances to hear Campbell's preaching, and a great many of them were converted to Christ.[6]

A few miles from the scene of Campbell's fervent preaching (also on the north side of the Clyde River) lived a young woman named Isabella Campbell whose two-story stone farmhouse was located at Fernicarry at the north end of the Gare Loch.[7] For a long time Isabella had been an invalid. She loved to discuss the things of the Lord with her many visitors, who often spoke of her saintly life and of her words which seemed to be uttered under the impulse of the Spirit. Her pastor, the Rev. Robert Story, whose church was in the nearby town of Rosneath, later wrote *Peace in Believing, or Memoirs of Isabella Campbell* (1829), an account of her ecstatic communion with the Lord.[8] Thousands of copies of this book were sold within a few weeks.

The first person we know of who experienced supernatural vision or revelation in the period just before 1830 was a James Grubb who lived on the south bank of the Clyde. Norton's narrative of Grubb and various related events is as follows:

> In the year 1828 died in that town [Port Glasgow] a poor man named Grubb. He had lived an irreligious life, but on his death-bed his penitence, and faith, and communion with God were most remarkable. "I shall never (writes one) forget the first time that I saw James Grubb, so extraordinary was the sight; the more than earthly brightness of his countenance. I had never seen anything so beautiful. —When he spoke there was such solemnity about him, that I felt quite awed in his presence, as if he were almost more than mortal. Often would he speak to my brothers and to others in a way they felt to be the Lord speaking through him. At other times—indeed at almost all times, if any one were present to whom he did not feel drawn in spirit, or taught of the Lord respecting them—he would scarcely utter a

word. He spoke much of the nearness of the Lord's coming; indeed, he seemed to have been taught of God every revealed truth, so as to cause Mr. —— to remark, 'Here is a man who a few weeks ago knew nothing, and now knows far more than all of us.'" His master thus wrote of him:—"His Bible was his constant companion; I think, I never called that I did not find it either in his hand, or on his pillow; and his wife has told me that while others slept, his nights were often spent in searching the word of God. His bedside was the school of Christ to many. He often spoke as one having authority, and knew that it was so; and for him to pray, and to receive the thing he prayed for, seemed almost one and the same thing."

According to another informant he had a remarkable vision or revelation, the particulars of which he never made known, but told his master Mr. Johnstone, that before his (Mr. Johnstone's) death, he also should be made to know it, and that his death would take place very soon; and he said enough to show that it referred to some great work of God about to appear in the Church. When Mr. Johnstone was dying the following summer [1829], he shouted out, "Now I know the mighty secret." Moreover, an old saintly woman, on being told of his dangerous illness, replied, "Ye little ken what wonderful things are connected with his death; but wait and ye shall see." And they did see; for the period of his death was the commencement of the outpouring of the Spirit on his native town and its neighborhood.

"There appeared about this time," says a third writer [Edward Irving], "in the deathbed experience of certain holy persons, very wonderful instances of the power of God's Spirit. In one instance the countenance shone with a glorious brightness. They spake much of a bright dawn about to arise in the Church; and one of them just before death signified that he had received the knowledge of the thing that was about to be manifested, but he was too far gone to give it utterance." The persons here referred to were James Grubb, Mr. Johnstone, his sister, and Isabella Campbell, of whom another writer informs us that (during the last year of her life) she was apparently so filled with the Holy Ghost that she dwelt rather in heaven than on earth, and it is stated by several that there were visible manifestations of glory in her appearance! [9]

After the death of these persons, their "mantle" seems to have fallen upon Mary Campbell in Fernicarry, and the Macdonald family in Port Glasgow. The Macdonalds for some time had been members of the established Church of Scotland (Presbyterian), but in addition had also been holding private prayer meetings of great length and fervor, being concerned with the salvation of their neighbors and the world at large.

Things were about the same until the spring of 1830. At that time, as Norton tells it, Margaret "had become increasingly an invalid, and was thought to be dying; when all at once she received the gift of prophecy." [10] It was on a certain morning in early 1830 [11] while confined to a sick bed in her house in Port Glasgow that Margaret had a most remarkable experience. Afterwards she wrote down a narrative of it entitled: "Recollections of the first morning of the outpouring of the Spirit." [12] Norton writes: "How little designed to be displayed, and therefore how unvarnished a narrative it is, may be inferred from the circumstance of its being now for the first time made public, after an interval of ten years. I will only premise that the writer of it had been, at the time referred to, confined to a sick bed for eighteen months, with no other expectation or desire than that of departing to be with Christ." [13]

Margaret's lengthy narrative, as published by Norton in 1840, is as follows:

"Throughout the morning I had felt very unwell, and disinclined to converse with any one; so much so that when Mrs. —— called as usual to inquire for me, I wished not to see her, and told her I was not able to talk with her, but she might pray. A few verses of the 106th psalm were sung: while singing that part of it 'His tender mercy doth endure,' &c. I was quite overpowered with a sense of the presence of God, and constrained to cry out, 'Eternity, eternity will never unfold its depth.' Immediately I was so swallowed up in God I did not see those who were with me in the room, nor hear their voices singing, but I heard the trump of God sounding in my ears so loud that all other sounds were lost. Indeed I heard unutterable things: the sound of the trumpet seemed to wax louder and louder as if that moment the Lord was to have been revealed. I felt surrounded by the heavenly hosts, a multitude which no man could number, and heard them singing 'Alleluia, for the Lord God omnipotent reigneth.' Oh, it was a blessed sound, and I felt constrained to join with them, and sing loudly the same glorious song. I did not feel on this earth—I thought it had vanished at the presence of the Lord. In spirit I saw the Lord coming in the glory of his Father and of all the holy angels, so that I was quite swallowed up in transport. I thought I had just to open my eyes and see the King in his beauty. No language can express the glorious things which were made to pass before me, nor the power with which they were brought to me. I was constrained to cry out for a speedy revelation of the glory that all flesh might see it. I felt there was indeed a weight of glory, and a need be that we should be changed in order to bear it. While I was desiring so much the speedy arrival of the day of the Lord, that passage 'God so loved the world,' &c. was powerfully impressed on me, and that the long suffering of God is salvation, not willing that any should perish. I felt that the spirit of Jesus was weeping, the same as he did over Jerusalem, over the world which was daring him to his face. But the unbelief of the world seemed nothing in comparison of the cold-hearted indifference of the people of God to the souls of men perishing around them, whilst Jesus was longing with an intense desire to make himself known to them. I saw the want of the mind of Christ in an awful manner, and how the Spirit was grieved in them, as if they hindered the work of God and the coming of Christ; seeing that nothing kept back his appearing but that souls might be brought in. I heard as it were the Spirit saying 'O will ye not ask that I may give life to dead souls.' A great many passages were brought to me about the willingness of God to give whatever we would ask; it was as if Jesus stood saying 'Ask that ye may receive,' and I was constrained to cry to those who were with me to ask for souls to be brought to Jesus. I felt the love of God to the world in a way I had never done before, and that Jesus, the same yesterday, to-day, and forever, was longing over souls with an intensity of love altogether inconceivable. It appeared so awful that his people should be so little of one spirit with Him, instead of crying night and day for them, seeing that the day of salvation would so soon be over; and that it was the unbelief and limiting of God which his own people were guilty of, which hindered mighty works from being done. I was made to cry much that there might be a great ingathering before the day of the Lord. Whilst so doing the ministers who are now preaching and writing against the truth, were brought before me as standing in the way. No language can express the agony of spirit I felt. The passages in the prophets where woes are denounced against unfaithful pastors, were brought before me as awful truths. The words 'Hell hath enlarged her mouth' were all I could utter. I wondered we could cease crying for mercy for them.

That passage in the thirty sixth Psalm 'Thy mercy Lord is in the heavens,' was given me, and I was enabled to cast them at the feet of Jesus, and to plead that they might be willing to become fools that they might be wise. Mr. C. [Rev. John McLeod Campbell] was brought before me as persecuted by these men, with the words 'Touch not mine anointed.' I was made to cry for strength for him, and while so doing, the passage in the fifty first of Isaiah, 'Art thou not it which hath dried the sea,' &c. was brought with great power. All the mighty works which God did for his anointed people passed before me. I was astonished and overwhelmed. But Oh I saw as if God were not known by his people. There seemed to be no faith on the earth. The eyes of God's people seemed so blinded by ignorance and unbelief. Abraham passed before me, and I saw that all were called to follow in his steps; but the falling away seemed very great. That passage in the fortieth of Isaiah 'He sitteth on the circle of the earth' &c. and many similar ones about the mighty majesty of God were brought to me. The world and all things in it seemed less than nothing and vanity, and it seemed so awful that those things which were soon to be swallowed up should blind the eyes of the people of God to those things which were so soon to be revealed. I felt that the spirit of God was greatly resisted by his people, and that nothing kept any one weak but unbelief. It seemed so awful that so little of his power was seen in his people, seeing He was the same, and his Spirit is not straitened. I saw that God was earnestly pleading with his people as a Father with his children, that all would be strong in faith giving him glory, but none seemed to listen to his voice. It seemed to me that christians were not at all alive; no one seemed to be under the power of the world to come, to see things as they were, or to believe that the day of the Lord was at hand. I felt there was need they should be awakened, for fiery trials awaited them. At this time a great deal was given me to say to my brothers. —All things again passed from before me. I was overpowered by a sense of the spotless purity of God, and saw that He is indeed a holy holy God who cannot look upon sin without abhorrence. Everything seemed black and desolate with it. A great many passages were pressed upon me, particularly that in Isaiah xxiv. 4–20, of the earth being defiled under its inhabitants, and the transgression thereof being heavy upon it. I shuddered and felt as if the whole creation groaned and travailed in pain. I saw that it was sin which marred the works of God, and had I not seen that Jesus on the cross had borne it away, I thought all must have sunk under it immediately. The price that had been paid in the sufferings of our Lord was brought before me, and I felt what an awful thing it was to have light views of sin. All his agony in the garden and on the cross went to my heart, and I was constrained to cry out 'Let every one that nameth the name of Christ depart from iniquity.' After this very much passed before me. I felt in a measure what it was to be come to the spirits of just men made perfect; I held intercourse and fellowship which I cannot describe, but which I knew to be reality." [14]

(Boase also describes a vision experienced by Mary Campbell in Fernicarry at about the same time and relates Rev. Story's eyewitness account of it.) [15]

Norton goes on to say that Margaret's brothers were far from any state of excited expectation, even after hearing about Margaret's experience, and things remained the same as before for nearly two months, until another morning similar to the one in February. Norton records a letter written by one of Margaret's older sisters,[16] telling about that later morning when Margaret underwent another outpouring of the Spirit, which was followed that same day by James' enduement of the Spirit and Margaret's healing, the news of

her healing reportedly resulting in Mary Campbell's healing
not long after.

Here is Norton's record of the older sister's letter:

"For several days —— [Margaret] had been so unusually ill
that I quite thought her dying, and on appealing to the doctor,
he held out no hope of her recovery unless she were able to go
through a course of powerful medicine, which he acknowledged
to be in her then case impossible. She had scarcely been able
even to have her bed made for a week. Mrs. —— and myself had
been sitting quietly at the bed-side, when the power of the Spirit
came upon her. She said 'there will be a mighty baptism of the
Spirit this day,' and then broke forth in a most marvellous
setting forth of the wonderful works of God, and as if her own
weakness had been altogether lost in the strength of the Holy
Ghost, continued with little or no intermission for two or three
hours, in mingled praise, prayer, and exhortation. At dinner-time
James and George came home as usual, whom she then
addressed at great length, concluding with a solemn prayer for
James that he might *at that time* be endowed with the power of
the Holy Ghost. Almost instantly James calmly said, 'I have got
it.' He walked to the window and stood silent for a minute or
two. I looked at him and almost trembled, there was such a
change upon his whole countenance. He then with a step and
manner of the most indescribable majesty, walked up to ——'s
[Margaret's] bed-side, and addressed her in those words of the
twentieth psalm, 'arise and stand upright.' He repeated the
words, took her by the hand, and she arose; when we all quietly
sat down and took our dinner. After it my brothers went to the
building yard as usual, where James wrote over to Miss C——
[Mary Campbell] commanding her in the name of the Lord to
arise. The next morning, after breakfast James said, I am going
down to the quay to see if Miss —— [Mary Campbell] is come
across the water: at which we expressed our surprise, as he had
said nothing to us of having written to her. The result showed
how much he knew of what God had done and would do for her,
for she came as he expected, declaring herself perfectly whole.
Rumour of all that had passed soon got abroad, and for two
days our house was scarcely ever empty of visitors. Satan alas
was busy also, trying to create confusion, and mar the work of

God, and unhappily too far succeeded in some, to our grief but especially that of James, than whom no one could more anxiously watch against the minglings of the devil and the flesh." [17]

Norton says that "a few evenings after the above occurrences, during a prayer meeting, George, in whom nothing supernatural had ever previously appeared, and whose natural caution had made him the last of the family to welcome the supernatural manifestations in others, began suddenly to speak in an unknown tongue; James followed him; and thus commenced, that speaking with tongues and prophesying which never afterwards wholly ceased." [18]

He then shares a letter written by James Macdonald on Tuesday, April 20, 1830, in which James reveals that he and his brother first spoke with unknown tongues on the previous Friday, April 16.[19] Although Margaret's friend, Mary Campbell, was the first person to speak with unknown tongues (on Sunday evening, March 28, 1830), there is no mention anywhere that Margaret did so before her brothers.

Since Norton declares that Margaret had her pre-trib revelation on "an evening" [20] (but does not specify which evening), and since Boase points out that both Margaret and Mary Campbell were dangerously sick during the time of their visions and revelations, it is safe to conclude that Margaret had her pre-trib revelation on some particular evening between February 1 and April 14.[21]

Margaret's prophetic ideas soon began affecting those around her. In the April 20 letter already mentioned, James Macdonald writes:

On Saturday Mr. C. [Rev. John McLeod Campbell] came over, and my mouth was again opened. He said, it is written 'pray that ye may interpret;' he accordingly prayed. I was then made to speak in short sentences which George interpreted one by one. The first word of interpretation was 'Behold he cometh—Jesus cometh.' [22]

In a letter dated April 19, 1830, R. B. Lusk of Greenock writes:

"I went up on Saturday evening, but on my arrival I found Mary Campbell and some of the rest of them on the quay, waiting for the steamboat to take them home. She appeared to be well, but thin. She said she was perfectly well. I walked about with her, conversing, for about ten minutes. She was calm and composed, apparently under no excitement, not ignorant of the peculiar desire of Satan to which they were exposed, and of the great necessity of being sober and watchful unto prayer . . . ."

"I afterwards saw Margaret M'Donald, and Mrs. Johnston, the widow of our late beloved brother. They both appeared to be in a state of strong excitement. I have never seen anything at all like Mrs. Johnston's appearance—I cannot describe it. But were it not that her words were words of truth, and that I had previously heard what I have now mentioned, I would have supposed her mad. The words she spoke were words of great power, and she seemed in an agony for utterance. I have omitted to mention that the burden of all they say is—that the Lord is near, near at hand." [23]

A letter written on May 18, 1830, by Mary Macdonald, Margaret's older sister, is as follows:

"What wonderful things have taken place among us since I last wrote you. Well may we exclaim, O what a God is our God—so very near to us his sinful rebellious creatures. Now in these last days He hath poured out his spirit, and is willing, most willing, to pour it out abundantly would we open our mouths to receive it. I have thought of writing you every day for some time, but ever since —— [Margaret, according to Boase, p. 765] was raised and the gift of tongues given, the house has been filled with people every day from all parts of England, Scotland, and Ireland; some of them are people inquiring what they must do to be saved, but the greater part are christians come to glorify God by witnessing what great things the Lord is doing amongst us; and there are a few who have come to dispute and deny the gifts. May the Lord be glorified in all and the creature abased. James would tell you about the gifts. One night at a prayer-meeting two persons were brought to know the Lord, and are going on making progress in the life of God. Last Wednesday the gift of tongues was given to Miss ——, and on Friday to our servant [Margaret Dewar, according to Boase, p. 766].

Last Saturday night after James had spoken in the tongues for a while, he prayed for interpretation, and the parable in Luke xix. of the nobleman going into a far country to receive a kingdom and to *return,* was given as the interpretation. It is very striking that almost all that has been interpreted has been on the coming of Christ.

There have been two more persons brought to know the Lord; one of them a child between five and six years of age. The Lord is carrying on a great work in this place, but the enemy is raging. Oh, you can have no idea how much we need your prayers and the prayers of all the people of God. The pulpits and newspapers are all against us, but greater is He that is with us than all that can be against us. Who can curse whom the Lord has blessed? The Lord reigneth: Jesus our elder brother is Head over all things to his body the church; all power in heaven and in earth is committed to Him; therefore will we trust and not be afraid." [24]

All during the late spring and summer months of 1830 Margaret's pre-trib views were being circulated at the many prayer and praise meetings that were held in various towns in western Scotland.

One who went up to Scotland to see things for himself was John B. Cardale who, on November 16, 1830, wrote to the editor of *The Morning Watch* an account of his observations the preceding August. In late 1972 I purchased a copy of Cardale's letter at the Catholic Apostolic Church Library in London's Gordon Square. Here are some parts of this document having to do with Margaret and her views:

We spent three weeks (some of us upwards of a month), arriving in the latter end of August, in Port-Glasgow and the neighbourhood, and attended regularly while there at the prayer-meetings; which meetings were held every evening, and occasionally (those only attending who were not engaged in business) in the morning. . . . Mrs. ——, one of the ladies who had received the Spirit, but had not received the gift of tongues (she received the gift while we were in the country), arose, went out of the room, and began speaking in a loud voice of the coming judgments. After she had spoken about five minutes, M. M'D. commenced also speaking, and Mrs. —— instantly ceased speaking. It is impossible to describe the solemnity and grandeur, both of words and manner, in which she gave testimony to the judgments coming on the earth; but also directed the Church to the coming of the Lord as her hope of deliverance. . . .[25]

The prayer-meetings are strictly private meetings, and for prayer. The rules they lay down for themselves do not allow of exposition, but simply the perusal of Scripture.

During our stay, four individuals received the gift of tongues; of these, two, Mrs. —— and M. M'D., had repeatedly spoken in the Spirit previously to their receiving the gift of tongues. . . .[26]

Whatever might have been the apparent exertion employed, I repeatedly observed that it had no exhausting effect upon them; that neither loudness of voice nor vehemence of action discomposed or exhausted them. And we had a remarkable instance of this in M. M'D. who one morning, having in consequence of a severe cold, so entirely lost the use of her voice as to be unable to speak out of a whisper, yet on a sudden commenced, and from 10 a.m. to 2 p.m. continued speaking in a loud voice—sometimes in intercessory prayer in the Spirit, sometimes in denouncing the coming judgments, and occasionally speaking in an unknown tongue—and at the end of that time she relapsed exactly into her former state, neither better nor worse than she had been in the morning, but without the slightest exhaustion from her long-continued efforts. . . .

In addition to what I have already stated, I have only to add my most decided testimony, that, so far as three weeks' constant communication, and the information of those in the neighbourhood, can enable me to judge (and I conceive that the opportunities I enjoyed enabled me to form a correct judgment), the individuals thus gifted are persons living in close communion with God, and in love towards Him, and towards all men; abounding in faith and joy and peace; having an abhorrence of sin, and a thirst for holiness, with an abasement of self, and yet with a hope full of immortality, such as I never witnessed elsewhere, and which I find no where recorded but in the history of the early Church: and just as they are fervent in spirit, so are they diligent in the performance of all the relative duties of life. They are totally devoid of any thing like fanaticism or enthusiasm; but, on the contrary, are persons of great simplicity of character, and of sound common sense. They have no fanciful theology of their own: they make no pretensions to deep knowledge: they are the very opposite of sectarians, both in conduct and principle: they do not assume to be teachers: they are not deeply read; but they seek to be taught of God, in the perusal of, and meditation on, His revealed word, and to "live quiet and peaceable lives in all godliness and honesty."

In giving you this statement in answer to your request, I am only fulfilling the duty of an honest man; for, with my conviction on this matter, I cannot but testify, in all proper places and times, the things which I have heard and seen: and may God bless my testimony to all to whom it may please Him that I should be enabled to give it, that He may be glorified, and His truth established!

Another letter written about 1834 by Francis Sitwell [27] to his sister, Mary, shows again the influence of Margaret's pre-trib views upon others. In it he says:

In consequence of some stories told me of our brethren concerning the Lord's people in Glasgow, I determined not to take any report, but go down and judge for myself, and I went to Edinburgh and got a letter of introduction from Mr. Pitcairn to the Macdonalds, and proceeded on to Port Glasgow. I arrived there a short time before dinner, and they received me kindly and asked me to stop. As soon as they sat down, the Spirit came upon the two brethren, and they returned thanks in the power of the Holy Ghost, and as soon as they ceased the word of the Lord came through Margaret Macdonald to the following effect to me. "Thou art a *pillar,* a child of God, a joint heir with Christ. Thou art a blood bought servant, be a faithful witness, be holy." You will see the reason why I mark the word "pillar" when we come to speak further on of what has been brought to pass, since you must remember Macdonald was a total stranger to me, and I to her, and could in no way know anything about me. Well, I stayed with them a few days, and the more I saw of the holiness of the people and of the character of the work (Do men gather grapes of thorns or figs of thistles?) the more was the conviction brought upon my mind, that the work was of God, indeed the details given to me by the Macdonald's of the commencement of the work, put the thing beyond a doubt, which details, without their permission, I do not feel myself at liberty to narrate, not that I conceive there would be any objection, but that I look upon private conversation as sacred without the express permission of the individual. . . .

All have proved to me the truth of the word that was forcibly impressed upon my mind the day I went to Port Glasgow. "That thou art my hiding place, Thou shalt preserve me from trouble, Thou shalt compass me about with songs of deliverance. I will instruct thee and teach thee in the way thou shalt go, I will guide thee with mine eye, Be ye not as horse or mule which have not understanding."

The very last portion of Sitwell's letter plainly expresses Margaret's pre-trib views and reveals his acceptance of them:

And now Mary I have given you this imperfect outline of my God's wondrous and merciful dealings with me, the most worthless sinner to whom ever grace and pardoning mercy was extended; and all the men in the world may rise up and cry delusion, fanaticism, imposture, yet I will (by grace) believe my God's guidance in all this and wait patiently upon Him that He may carry on His work in His own way and perfect that which concerneth us and maketh us ready for His appearing. And why do I write this to you? Is it to gratify your curiosity? No! it is to show you in all this I have not acted inadvisedly, nor rashly, but patiently, yielding myself to the guidance of the Lord. It is because I am anxious if possible, to remove prejudice out of your mind. It is because I believe the time of Babylon's destruction draweth nigh. It is because I love you and John that you also should flee out while *yet* there is time, while yet there is mercy (But he seemed as one that mocked unto his son's in law Gen. xix 14). It is because the time of the worlds doom draweth nigh, it is because the time of sealing is come, it is because the Lord is nigh, even at the door. It is because there is no safety where you are, because you cannot be sealed where you are, it is because if you are not sealed you must be left in the tribulations, while those who have obeyed His voice shall be caught up to meet Him. It is because of these things and because I love you, that I have written to you so large a letter with my own hand, and I commend it unto the Lord's hand, I pray Him to bless it to you, to John and Anna. It is for his glory I have written it. May His own good will and pleasure be done with it, it is useless to multiply words. May grace and mercy and peace be yours etc etc.

We have seen in this chapter that there were developing ideas which undoubtedly "set the stage" for Margaret's pronouncement, that Margaret's pre-trib revelation occurred sometime in the early part of 1830 *before* she and her brothers ever spoke in unknown tongues, that her views were being circulated in her hometown of Port Glasgow soon after her revelation and healing, and that the unknown tongues did not *create* her views but rather *emphasized* them (as they also emphasized established doctrines such as salvation).

The tongues, therefore, were a separate item and should not be lumped together with the origin and formulation of the pre-trib school of interpretation. (I know many charismatic persons today who are post-tribs and, on the other hand, many pre-tribs who definitely are not charismatic.)

If Margaret's pre-trib rapture views did not spring from the unknown tongues of her time, as some have concluded, was she persuaded only by her examination of Scripture?

What kind of persons were the Macdonalds and what can be known about them?

NOTES

1. On the cover of Boase's work, which is a supplement to his larger volume entitled *The Elijah Ministry* (1868), are the words "Printed for Private Circulation." Charles William Boase was born in London on June 8, 1804, joined the C.A.C. in 1836, was ordained to the priesthood in October of the same year, and ordained to the episcopate in August

of 1851. He wrote several volumes and pamphlets and died at Albury in Surrey on June 7, 1872, the day before his sixty-eighth birthday.

2. Such as Isa. 32:15; Joel 2:23, 28; and Zech. 10:1.

3. Stewart was one of those attending the first Albury conference in 1826.

4. Row at that time was a popular bathing resort located about five miles west of the banks of Loch Lomond. (See Norton's *Memoirs*, p. 62.)

5. Norton, *Restoration*, p. 3, states that those who rejoiced in Campbell's truths included "the sisters of Isabella Campbell [no known relation], of Fernicarry, and a family of the name of Macdonald, the heads of which were two brothers, shipbuilders in Port-glasgow." Later, in 1831, the local presbytery deposed Campbell for his "heretical" views.

6. *Op. Cit.*, p. 753.

7. Today that small village is called Garelochhead. The Campbell home, in which Darby stayed several days as an observer of the 1830 charismatic manifestations, was built in 1780 and is still standing. On a cold, rainy afternoon late in 1972 we chatted in the living room with the present occupants, Mrs. Jessie Stark and Mrs. Margaret Fraser, and also discovered a monument to Isabella on the hill behind the house on which were chiseled these words: HERE ISABELLA CAMPBELL WAS WONT TO PRAY.

8. There is no record, however, that she ever spoke in unknown tongues; the first known case of tongues-speaking in the 1830 charismatic revival (according to an article on Irving in the *Dictionary of National Biography*, 1963–64, Vol. X, p. 491, and other sources) involved Isabella's sister, Mary, who first spoke in tongues while on a bed of sickness on Sunday evening, March 28, 1830. Story says Isabella died on Nov. 1, 1827, at 20 years of age; he told other attendants at the second Albury conference in late 1827 about her remarkable life and death.

9. Norton, *The Restoration* . . . . , pp. 3–5. It should be mentioned that Irving preached the imminent second coming in Edinburgh, Glasgow, Rosneath, Row, and other cities and towns in Scotland in the summer of 1828, and that Rev. Alexander J. Scott, a young missionary of the Church of Scotland who later became Irving's assistant in London, preached on the outpouring of the Spirit and manifestation of gifts, in Greenock and vicinity in the fall of 1829, and undoubtedly influenced those involved in the following year's outburst. Scott, however, disapproved of later manifestations in Irving's London congregation though he was still his assistant.

10. *Ibid.*, p. 6. In his *Memoirs*, p. 101, Norton describes Margaret as "the first individual upon whom, as I believe, the Spirit of prophecy fell, and the only one who appears to have committed to writing an account of their first experience of its power sufficiently detailed to enable a spiritual reader to form some judgment on the subject . . ." (See also his *Neglected and Controverted Scripture Truths*, pp. 392–393.)

11. Boase (*op. cit.,* pp. 756, 758) dates this experience as on or about Feb. 1, 1830.
12. Norton, *Memoirs*, p. 101.
13. *Ibid.,* p. 101.
14. *Ibid.,* pp. 101–107. Boase, *(op. cit.)* pp. 758–759, quotes portions of Norton's inclusion of it in his *Memoirs.*
15. Pp. 756–758. He says that both Mary and Margaret had visions and revelations during their time of illness, that their revelations were similar, and that some of them were recorded. He describes their physical and mental condition during a vision or revelation: "a state of bodily syncope during which the spirit was in an ecstasy literally indescribable; then of slight bodily revival, during which the soul seemed to see and hear things of which an account could be given; then a return to full consciousness to things around, with ability to speak to those present."
16. Revealed in Boase, p. 759, as Mary Macdonald. He dates her letter Wednesday, April 14, 1830.
17. *Memoirs*, pp. 107–109.
18. *Ibid.,* p. 110.
19. *Ibid.,* p. 111.
20. *Restoration*, p. 15.
21. The evening in question took place in March of 1830, according to Anderson's *Heralds of the Dawn*, p. 40, and Edwards' *The Day of Vengeance*, p. 29, but neither author offers proof.
22. Norton, *Memoirs*, p. 111.
23. Boase, pp. 763–764.
24. Norton, *Memoirs*, pp. 125–126.
25. Boase, p. 779, and Norton, *Restoration*, p. 23, include this portion of Cardale's letter. In Norton's book the last sentence reads: "It is impossible to describe the solemnity and grandeur both of words and manner in which Miss M—— gave testimony to the judgments coming on the earth, but also directed the Church to the coming of the Lord as her hope of deliverance."
26. Cardale thus reveals that Margaret received the gift of tongues either in August or September of 1830.
27. Boase, p. 814, says Sitwell became one of the twelve Apostles of the Catholic Apostolic Church in 1835. On p. 826 he writes: "During the meeting of the thirteenth monthly Council, in June 1836, the second called Apostle, speaking in the power of the Holy Ghost, was made to declare that the Lord would divide Christendom among the Apostles, the princes of the tribes of Israel. And the whole of the Continent of Europe was accordingly distributed into ten portions, to each of which an Apostle was assigned, while the two senior Apostles respectively were shewn that England, and Scotland with Switzerland, formed their tribes; thus bringing out the twelvefold character of the spiritual Israel,

answering to the twelve tribes in the Revelation, from among whom the sealed ones, the twelve thousand out of each tribe, should be gathered, who should be the first fruits to God and the Lamb." He adds that Sitwell was designated as Apostle over Spain and Portugal. (Francis V. Woodhouse was Apostle over America, then seen as "a suburb of Christendom.")

8. THE MACDONALD CLAN

Trying to dig out facts on the Macdonalds of Port Glasgow, Scotland, is inordinately difficult. One thing, however, is crystal clear, they certainly weren't publicity crazy. Again I am indebted to Norton for much of the content of this chapter. In his *Memoirs* he reports briefly on the early years of Margaret's two older brothers:

> The twin brothers James and George Macdonald, were born on the 11th of December 1800, at Saltcoats (on the western coast of Scotland), of which town their father Captain James Macdonald was one of the principal inhabitants, and a man singularly respected and beloved. There was nothing remarkable about their childhood or youth, except that their natural dispositions were peculiarly amiable, and their abilities so promising that their father designed them for some learned profession. His death however prevented this; and at the usual period they became fellow apprentices to a ship builder. On the expiration of their apprenticeship, they took a voyage to Calcutta, their friends thinking that their prospects would be more promising there; but disliking the country they returned to Scotland, and commenced business as ship builders at Port Glasgow, where they continued to live together until death separated them.[1]

While Norton does speak of the father of this family, he says nothing in his writings about Margaret's mother who apparently also died early in their lifetimes. The responsibilities of raising the three sisters[2] seem to have fallen upon the shoulders of the brothers, James and George.

A thorough search in the town of Port Glasgow for official records on the Macdonald family turned up nothing. A long walk through an old cemetery there was also fruitless (although the exercise gave us a craving for a tasty dinner of fish and chips). Everywhere we went in Port Glasgow and nearby Greenock we asked the people: "Have you ever heard of the Margaret Macdonald who was famous in this area around 1830?" The answer was always No.

We even put an ad in the Edinburgh *Scotsman*: "American wishes new information about Margaret Macdonald who lived in Port Glasgow in 1830." But there has never been even a single reply. Some of the natives suggested that we go to Edinburgh and look over old documents at the Register House. After days of painstaking scrutiny of thousands of pages of old parish records, we finally came upon an entry in faded ink which could well be Margaret's record of birth:

> James McDonald, joiner, in Port Glasgow, & Mary Ivory—daughter, Margaret, born Jan. 14, 1815, and baptized Jan. 22, 1815.[3]

Margaret's two brothers, while in their early manhood, evidently attempted to set up their own business enterprise which failed after one of them had a serious illness. This setback turned their thoughts to things spiritual and, as Norton tells it,

> they commenced the practice of family worship, reading morning and evening prayers, and gradually became very solicitous for an assurance of their interest in Christ: earnestly labouring after, yet ignorant how to obtain, that peace and joy which are to be found and only found in simply believing the gospel as a message to "every creature" that Christ loved him and gave himself for him.[4]

They continued in this state of mind until the spring of 1828. At that time James received Christ as his personal Saviour. A few weeks later George similarly opened his heart to the Lord and became a new creature in Christ. In the days to follow, Margaret's two older sisters, Mary and Jane, followed the brothers' examples and were converted also.

The lone holdout was the youngest sister, Margaret. Norton writes:

> The last who remained a miserable homeless wanderer about six months after the happy ingathering of her brothers, had been long looked up to by the rest as the most religious of them all; years of anxiety had she endured, spending her days and nights in seeking peace to her soul, traversing every bye-path and attempting every effort of self-righteousness, terminating only in deepening despair, until at last, even more instantaneously than had been the case with James, her eyes were opened upon her Saviour through the instrumentality of a most remarkable individual [James Grubb] . . . .[5]

Things were soon different in the Macdonald household. Whereas before their conversion the two brothers had been frequent guests at parties and other places of entertainment in town, now every evening found them eagerly reading the Bible and spending hours in prayer. And now the big word in their lives was love, love to Him who had first loved them.

Whether or not the second coming was then in James' thoughts, Norton says that

> James especially for months after his conversion was continually longing to depart and be with Christ. Once on some one mentioning a christian who had lived many years after being brought to the knowledge of God, he seemed overwhelmed with sorrow, and clasping his hands and looking up cried shall I be separated from my Jesus so long? One night, however, as they were lying awake talking as they continually did of Christ and of their longing to be with him, James felt that passage impressed upon him, "Let your light so shine before men that they may see your good works and glorify your Father which is in heaven;" and they accepted this as a sufficient reason why they should not be at once removed to their Father's home.[6]

In two important paragraphs Norton explains the extent of their knowledge of biblical doctrine and also tells about two preachers of that day, Campbell and Irving:

Their doctrinal knowledge was at first very limited; they knew little more than that Jesus was their Saviour, and that they loved him because he was such; thus, one night shortly after James's conversion, he was lying awake perplexed at his own ignorance, and wondering how he might be best taught and guided, when that passage was powerfully impressed upon him, "My God shall supply all your need, according to his riches in glory, by Christ Jesus." And truly remarkable and rare was the singleness of eye with which they waited for and depended on their heavenly Father's teaching. They procured no religious books; for years they scarcely read one; the ministry under which they sat was unimpressive; and if they did adopt peculiar views of divine truth, it was from no heretical writings or preaching but from the bible alone that they derived them.

For instance, although they soon became classed among the disciples of Mr. Irving, who was at that time beginning to be stigmatized as heretical, the fact was that, so far as I can ascertain, they never read a single volume of his, or at least not for years after their own views were established. And although after a time they began to attend the preaching of the Rev. Mr. Campbell of Row, whose deposition from the church and ministry for holding similar views will afterwards be noticed, it was because they had previously been taught of God the same truths, and were attracted to Row by their love to them. —Not, however, that they entirely agreed with all that either Mr. I. or Mr. C. preached and wrote. Far from it.[7]

Concerning the prophetic views held at that time by the Macdonald brothers (who probably influenced their sisters), Norton writes:

With respect to the doctrine of Christ's millennial advent and reign, I need scarcely explain how they came to adopt this, as it is a truth imprinted on the sacred page in characters of such vivid light, that the only wonder is that any simple minded child of God can be so blind as not to see it there.

Next, but almost last of all, they were led to see from scripture the perpetuity of the miraculous endowments of the church, and the consequent responsibility of the church for their disappearance and continued absence. Such were their distinguishing

views, and in the above order and way were they gradually led
into the adoption of them.[8]

Early in the summer of 1828, says Norton, James and
George met the ailing James Grubb and a short-lived
friendship was formed. That same summer the brothers
secured lodging for their sisters at Row, where Rev. John
McLeod Campbell preached to great crowds. Margaret, then
an invalid, accompanied her sisters. Her conversion was soon
to take place.

Norton explains the part James Grubb played in Margaret's decision to accept Christ, and includes a lengthy
account by an unnamed eyewitness:

A young lady who with her brothers was privileged to be a
frequent visitor of his, very naturally spoke to him of her
youngest sister [Margaret Macdonald] who had been long an
invalid and was staying for the summer at Row. It was
remarkable with how great eagerness the very first mention of
her case was received by him. From that time he seemed to bear
her on his heart before the Lord, and the Lord seemed to have
made known to him much more of her actual situation than was
known even to the members of her family. A day or two after,
taking the hand of one of her brothers while I also was sitting by,
he said with great solemnity, 'Your sister's bodily complaints are
the least of her diseases; her soul is diseased, and she is
departing from Christ the only physician.' Two days afterwards
the Lord afforded me an opportunity of becoming a witness to
the fact: I found she had been deeply pierced by a sermon she
had heard at Row the sabbath preceding, and that instead of
thankfully receiving the message of the gospel, her whole heart
was armed against it. But it was the same night that James had
been bearing her on his spirit in prayer, that the agony of her
mind was most remarkable. I saw her again some days afterwards, but still she seemed as far or farther from her Saviour
than ever. Her heart seemed cold, and a kind of settled
indifference was visible upon her very countenance. The same
evening her brothers came across; the subject of their converse
was chiefly the wonderful things which they had seen and heard

in their dying friend. Some of his sayings were repeated, and amongst them one which as one of the brothers said, had been ringing in his ears ever since he heard it. It was this, 'Jesus, Jesus, I have as good a right to Jesus, as if I had made Him.' [9] The wandering sheep had apparently been an unconcerned listener till now, but at these words was in an instant enabled to acknowledge and rejoice in the same Redeemer as hers. I shall never forget the knock that came to our door late that night; I opened it myself, and there stood before me a dear brother and sister, who at her earnest desire had travelled with full hearts to tell us what great things the Lord had done for them. We all went on our knees and gave the glory and the praise to God. For a great part of the night she continued in such a frame of spirit that with regard to much of it, one might apply to her the apostle's words and say, "Whether in the body or out of the body she could hardly tell." I saw her in the morning; all was peace and love and joy: such a contrast to what I had seen the day before I could hardly have conceived. Weak as she was, she was able to go to church, and there, laid on a stair with a pillow under her, drank deep of the water of life, where only a week before the same stream was to her as wormwood and gall. A few days after, she came across and was enabled to visit him more than once. [10]

As we saw in the last chapter, the Macdonalds at this time were conducting prayer meetings for special intercession. In several paragraphs Norton sheds more light on this closely-knit family of three sisters and two brothers:

But they were not sectarian or schismatic; they at the same time joined a prayer meeting which had been held for several years by a few of the principal religious characters of the town, and although they soon ceased to derive much enjoyment from it, yet for the sake of "endeavouring to keep the unity of the Spirit in the bond of peace," they would not willingly have separated themselves from it; but they were now beginning to be looked upon as heretical, and the increasing incongeniality of their views at length led the other members of it to request them to discontinue their attendance.

They also sought to connect themselves with the parochial

sabbath school, but for a similar reason were excluded from it also. They then attempted to form a sabbath school of their own, but the powerful influence which was exerted to dissuade parents from sending their children, limited it to a very few; still, small as it was, they continued it to the last.

Their own parish minister now began to preach vehemently against them, or at least against what were known to be their peculiar views of truth; but this only led them to prayer for him. An hour before the morning service was specially set apart for this purpose, also a similar though shorter period before the afternoon service.

They made repeated attempts to get the public newsroom closed on the Lord's day, and on the failure of their exertions withdrew from it. In every other way also they sought to manifest that they were on the Lord's side; still they studiously avoided, for they ever disliked, all barely external singularity, and every thing that could justly be deemed extravagant or bring reproach upon the truth; and thus, notwithstanding all the grievous doctrinal errors which they were imagined to hold, they continued to be universally acknowledged as blameless in all worldly things.

I believe the very worst fault laid to their charge was the rumour which got abroad, and which certainly was true, that they were occupied through the winter in converting their somewhat extensive library into fuel for the evening's fire; but this was because it principally consisted of the godless and therefore worthless productions of the great idols of our literature. They burned no religious books; they laid them away, however, with the exception of a few; still confining their reading almost exclusively to the bible; while of this it was indeed literally true that their delight was in the law of the Lord, and in his law did they meditate day and night.[11]

The events of the spring of 1830, including Margaret's pre-trib revelation, have already been presented. But what happened to this unusual family in the years that followed? Norton reports:

For the first few years, and almost until the last, more or less so, the happy quiet of their domestic circle was broken in upon by an almost continual succession of visitors. With the exceptions that this unavoidably occasioned, their private habits underwent no change; and I need scarcely add, that their holy walk with God underwent no deterioration in consequence of the miraculous gifts. To describe what they continued to be after this outpouring of the Spirit, would be a repetition of the description already given of their earlier life. There is however one point to which I may refer here as strikingly characterizing their latter years, viz., their reverence for the Lord's day. So extremely strict was their conscientious observance of it, that if, for instance, a letter from some dear christian friend happened to be handed to them during the Sabbath, they would lay it aside unopened till next morning; and little as it was that they at any time read out of other religious books than the bible, I believed that on the Lord's day they invariably confined their reading exclusively to *it*. I mention these supererogatory restrictions, not as necessary models for imitation, but simply to shew how very far they were from being lifted up by their gifts into any unholy or presumptuous liberty.

The two brothers still continued, after the outpouring of the Spirit, to attend as before their parish church, although continually alluded to and attacked in a very painful manner, and made the gaze of the whole congregation; but on the deposition of their friend the Rev. Mr. Campbell from his ministerial office in the Scotch church, they regarded this as virtually their own expulsion from it, and consequently resigned their membership in it. So far, however, were they from a schismatic spirit, that before they left the Scotch church they would, I believe, willingly have joined the church of England, had circumstances been favourable for their doing so; for they never encouraged any of its members who came to visit them,[12] to leave it; but the contrary. They could not indeed regard the existing ordinations as more than human and external, still they thought the Lord alone could substitute better, and that His time and way were to be waited for.[13]

After the Macdonalds left the Scotch church, they continued the practice of conducting prayer meetings in their own home and also added various church ordinances at these services. Not only did they open their house to outsiders but also hired a small chapel in a nearby town and for a while large crowds were in attendance at both places.[14]

Norton records a letter, written possibly by one of the older Macdonald sisters, describing one of the meetings in their home:

> "Our house is open every Wednesday and Sabbath, and George preaches: there is an immense crowd; the house and stairs crowded, and sometimes the street. The Lord generally confirms the word by his own Spirit, sometimes through George himself. The opposition is fearful. James preaches in Greenock. The Lord's presence has been much with him, and his word confirmed by the Spirit through Mrs.—— and ——. A few weeks ago the crowd was so great, around as well as within the house, that we had to go round and get in at a back door to the stair, where James stood, the doors and windows being open for the people in the street to hear. I never heard the gospel preached in such power. The next night, they found the door locked. There was an immense crowd, upwards of a thousand. James got a chair and stood on it under a lamp, and there proclaimed the gospel of the grace of God: the night was very wet and dark, yet the people stood all the time. The rage of some was fearful; they said James and —— should be dragged out of the town and this put an end to at once. The natural heart of man is the same as when they drew Paul out of the city, stoned him, and left him for dead. —Blessed be His name, 'tis enough that the disciple be as his master and the servant as his Lord." [15]

When a serious cholera epidemic began to take many lives in Great Britain in late 1831 and the months that followed, the Macdonalds ministered to many victims of the plague in their own neighborhood. As Norton tells it,

> One period of the ministerial labours of love of the two brothers, demanding special notice, is that of the prevalence of the Cholera. The ministers of the place, and of the neighbouring town, had long been most zealous in warning their flocks against them as dangerous men; but when the real danger came, almost all these shepherds, comparatively at least, contented themselves with leaving the multitude of perishing souls to die around them

unvisited. In Port-Glasgow almost the only individuals who would enter the houses of the sick, were the Macdonalds; while they devoted themselves day and night to such visits of mercy, not merely going wherever they were sent for, but seeking out neglected cases, and ministering both to the body and to the soul; and, not satisfied with this, James felt constrained to walk over weekly to the hospital in Greenock, and there minister from ward to ward to the neglected dying. Their christian devotedness at this period, and its contrast with the very opposite conduct of others, did not pass unnoticed, and almost universally secured for them, ever afterwards, at least a silent respect.[16]

Other insights into the private lives of the Macdonalds are included in Norton's writings. In *Memoirs* he devotes almost a page to some personal notations made by James:

We have already seen how the two brothers abounded in prayer; they no less gave themselves to fasting also, working out their salvation with fear and trembling, as knowing that they had not yet attained, neither were already perfect. Almost the only private papers of James's which remain, are some memorandums in one of his pocket-books, from which I extract the following diary of some of his fast days for 1833 and 1834, the two last years of his life.

January 1st, 1833.—Observed this day as a fast, but did not find much personal dealing with God.

March 26th.—Observed this day as a fast, and have cause to bless God for the measure of grace given to draw near to Him in any measure.

May 1st.—Observed this day as a fast, seeking to humble myself before the Lord: had cause of thanksgiving for the measure of peace and comfort granted; but did not find that measure of contrition and brokenness of spirit which was desirable.

July 16th.—Observed this day as a fast, but have cause of sorrow that I know so little of a fasting spirit, or of making confession of sins of heart, with that sorrow which worketh repentance.

January 1st, 1834.—Observed this day as a fast, and felt that the Lord acknowledged it.

September 3rd.—Observed this day as a day of fasting and humbling myself before the Lord.[17]

Oliphant, though seldom at a loss of words, has little by way of description of the Scottish family under consideration. But she does record that "the Macdonalds, less demonstrative, and more homely, went on upon their modest way, attracting crowds of observers, without being thereby withdrawn from the composed and sober course of their existence . . ." [18]

Whether the Macdonalds ever journeyed to London to see for themselves the manifestations in Irving's congregation is brought out by Norton, who reveals:

Another trait very illustrative of their character, and of the singleness of their heart and their motives, was the answer which they gave to the pressing invitations to them to go up to London, made by some of the affluent and influential members of Mr. Irving's congregation, who would doubtless have made most generous and honourable provision for them there. Such an invitation, which would have surrounded them with friends and admirers, must have attracted them had they been under the influence of worldly or ambitious motives, especially as their business, which through various losses and misfortunes had never been successful, was at that time, as indeed at all times, a most anxious, laborious, and inadequate source of maintenance, particularly as they were almost obliged to keep an open and hospitable house. Both the brothers however, ever declined going, simply because they could not see that the Lord was calling them there, and, as they said, felt it would be doubly inexcusable in *them* to run before Him.[19]

Not only is there no recorded instance of the Macdonalds going to London in connection with the charismatic revival, but there is evidence they opposed the later Irvingite manifestations. Norton includes an entire letter written from Port Glasgow by George Macdonald on May 8, 1832. In it he writes:

. . . although many things have taken place in London which we cannot explain, this does not stumble us as to the reality of the Lord's presence; neither though a prophet may have been deceived or spoken presumptuously, is it enough to prove that the work in him is all a delusion. . . .

That deceptions would be, was also to be expected, for where the Spirit of God is at work, there Satan is ever busiest, and generally finds means to hinder what the Lord would do. In looking back I cannot say I see no glory to God; I see much of the word opened up, and doctrines brought forward which have been much hid for ages. It is to try the faith of his people, and all who have been resting on an arm of flesh will be shaken and fall; whoever received it from Mr. Irving, Mr. Baxter,[20] or any other human authority will feel their foundation unstable; and the sooner they are brought to this, the better; there is no abiding but on the word of God, and against this nothing can prevail.[21]

After this letter Norton publishes another one, undated and written by James Macdonald. Touching upon the manifestations in Irving's church, he writes:

Now while it is plain that it could not be the Spirit of God which spoke anything false, yet we see it is possible that a true prophet may, through unguarded walking, be left to utter a vision of his own; both as a chastisement to himself, and to the people who may have been improperly looking to him. . . .

When we consider that the manifestation of the Spirit is the operation of another Person, viz. the Spirit, distinct from the individual in whom the operation is, we can see how a man may be ministering much edifying to the church, and yet be without the benefit of it himself. The person made use of is placed in the most favourable circumstances for profiting by it, yet sin may mar the most favourable circumstances. The Spirit of God however could not long continue in any one who was not profiting by his presence, or was indulging in any sin, whether pride or vain-glory, or any other. It may be, (and is it to be wondered at?) that such a person should be ready to receive and utter vain and foolish things, and go farther and farther into error and darkness, until he may be so far from the light of God's presence as to be unable to discern what he formerly was assured of.[22]

Throughout the fall of 1834 James exhibited symptoms of what the author-doctor describes as "incipient pulmonary disease." In the following winter he wrote what Norton says was his last letter, which contained the following lines: "My illness has been a time of much comfort. God has never left me in it; but said unto me continually, I am thy God." [23] James' last day on earth is described several pages later:

> In the course of the morning many came to see him, to almost all of whom he addressed some word in season; but at length he ceased to speak and lay still, occasionally smiling. In this state he continued until near four in the afternoon, when being raised that he might take some wine, he just looked up—his whole face brightened with a smile of joy—he quietly laid his head on his brother's shoulder, and expired; on the second day of February, 1835. A cry of agony escaped from his desolate brother as the liberated spirit fled; but soon all knelt down in thanksgiving and praise to Him who had taken to himself so dear a brother and friend. [24]

Several months after James' departure George contracted the same consumption that had afflicted his brother. [25] Norton portrays the end:

> A smile of far more than merely human brightness shone upon his face; his eyes were intensely riveted on some most glorious Object; he stretched out his arms, gradually raised himself on his bed, as if pressing toward the bright object on which they were fixed, and with whose brightness they were unutterably kindled, then he cried, Lift me up nearer, nearer, nearer to Jesus. He shortly became exhausted, and a period of agony came on, during which he tried in vain to give utterance to his feelings; but after a short distressing struggle, he gained the victory, and fell asleep—on the fourteenth day of September 1835. [26]

The only reference to Margaret's death is found in Norton's *Restoration* in two sentences telling about the death of her brothers:

> Not long afterwards, with a short interval between each other, these two brothers,—and a few years afterwards their sister,—

fell asleep in Jesus. She ere her own departure, as her husband [27] here bears testimony, in perfect peace and never-varying assurance of God's presence, and with the words of the Psalmist, "Joy cometh in the morning" on her lips . . .[28]

While doing research for this book at Glasgow's Mitchell Library in 1972, my wife and I were allowed to examine old issues of the Glasgow *Herald.* We found brief announcements of the deaths of both Macdonald brothers.

The Monday, February 9, 1835, edition stated concisely:

> At Port-Glasgow, on the 2d instant, of consumption, aged 34 years, Mr. James M'Donald, shipbuilder.

George's death notice, found in the Monday, September 21, 1835, *Herald,* read simply:

> At Port-Glasgow, on the 14th inst., of consumption, Mr. George M'Donald, shipbuilder.

Somewhere in this big world there must be some more old documents throwing further light on Miss Margaret Macdonald and her pre-trib revelation of 1830. Maybe this book will encourage someone to search for them. And then share them.

NOTES

1. Pp. 48–49. James apparently was born first; he is often mentioned as the elder brother. James also died first.
2. William F. MacArthur's *History of Port Glasgow* (1932), in the Port Glasgow Public Library, says James and George had three sisters. Mary Macdonald was included in the preceding chapter, and Norton, p. 234, gives the third sister's name as Jane.
3. *Parochial Register (Port Glasgow, 1804–1819)*, p. 893, found at Register House, Edinburgh. If this is Margaret's actual birth record, she was fifteen when she had her pre-trib revelation. Other records at this facility fixed Port Glasgow's population in 1830 as approximately 5,100 persons.
4. P. 50.
5. Pp. 55–56.

6. P. 57.
7. Pp. 58–59.
8. Pp. 60–61.
9. At this point Norton adds a footnote: "Let not this expression offend any one, but its seeming rudeness be placed to the rudeness of his previous life and habits of speech, when we see that God who looketh at the heart, and knew that his servant was only labouring to express his sense of His unspeakable *gift,* was pleased to make it the channel of conveying to another soul the saving knowledge of Christ."
10. Pp. 68–70.
11. Pp. 75–77.
12. Norton, an Anglican, may have been referring to himself here.
13. Pp. 178–179.
14. P. 184.
15. Pp. 185–186. When in Port Glasgow late in 1972 we were unable to discover the Macdonald house and found no record of its location. This vital shipbuilding town was heavily bombed in World War II, and current plans for shipyard expansion may soon level many more old houses in the center of town.
16. Pp. 197–198.
17. P. 197.
18. *The Life of Edward Irving,* pp. 289–290.
19. *Memoirs,* pp. 198–199.
20. This was Robert Baxter, author of *Narrative of Facts* (1833). More about him later.
21. *Memoirs,* pp. 203–204.
22. Pp. 205–207.
23. P. 233.
24. P. 237.
25. Like Isabella Campbell, both Macdonald brothers died of the same consumptive disease of which Mary Campbell claimed to have been healed.
26. P. 244. Norton says in his *Restoration,* p. 38, that he was also present at George's bedside when he passed away.
27. Norton does not reveal the identity of Margaret's husband. In *Memoirs,* p. 247, he speaks of a family brother-in-law, John G. Hamilton, but does not say which Macdonald sister was his wife.
28. P. 36. On p. 87, he says Mary Campbell died in 1840. (Shortly after her healing she had married W. R. Caird, a law clerk.)

9. HOW HIDDEN IT WAS!

The first words of the first chapter of Robert Norton's *The Restoration of Apostles and Prophets; In the Catholic Apostolic Church* are these:

> The work which God hath wrought in these last days, in preparation for the coming and kingdom of His Son, our Lord and Saviour Jesus Christ, has been generally known, or rather has remained unknown, under the false designation of Irvingism; whereby its true origin and character have been hidden and misrepresented. The name of Edward Irving is worthy of perpetual remembrance and honour, inasmuch as he was the first minister who publicly recognized it; and he devoted his whole after life, with a martyr's self-sacrifice, to its maintenance and progress.[1]

In this important statement Norton says that Irvingism's "true origin and character have been hidden and misrepresented." When Norton wrote these words in 1861 he was well aware that the real originator of the pre-trib rapture theory—Margaret Macdonald—had been forgotten by or was unknown to many evangelical believers outside the ranks of the Catholic Apostolic Church. And since he had been an eyewitness of the 1830 charismatic revival in western Scotland and had known the Macdonalds and carefully recorded their views, he was compelled in later years to reveal Margaret as the one whose views he had already published in his earliest writings.[2] Not only has the true pre-trib origin been hidden for a long time, but much of the Catholic

Apostolic Church literature, including Norton's books and pamphlets, has long been hibernating in places of cloistered seclusion.

P. E. Shaw, an expert on Irvingite history, writes:

> The literature of the [Catholic Apostolic] Church, chiefly pamphlets, is vast. Some is only for private circulation, but since it is now possible to obtain it from secondhand booksellers it may be assumed that the privacy of a hundred years ago no longer holds. Much of it is almost inaccessible or may be purchased only at prices practically prohibitive; and probably much has never been made public or is hidden away from the merely curious. Most of it is anonymous, which, while not impairing its devotional value for the faithful, makes it difficult for others to estimate its historical value; but by the aid of library catalogues and other means at the writer's disposal the names of some of the authors have been traced, and are given in parentheses.[3]

The many observers of the 1830 charismatic revival were well aware of Margaret's pre-trib rapture views, as I have been careful to point out. Anyone visiting the Macdonald home in Port Glasgow at that time knew that her interpretation of prophecy was the central theme of the manifestations. Though it is unthinkable that anyone could have visited the Macdonalds and gone away with no knowledge of her views, yet the fact remains that many outsiders who did not personally investigate the happenings knew only of the reports of tongues and healing and other miraculous and spectacular events. So, in a very real way, the pre-trib origin was hidden even to many of Margaret's contemporaries.

The newspapers and other publications of the day generally seized upon the "showy" things and quietly ignored (and probably were unaware of) the strong, underlying apocalyptic theme that permeated those things. On one wall of my study hangs a photocopy of the front page of the Friday, June 18, 1830, Glasgow *Herald* which features an article entitled "The Row Heresy and Gairloch Miracles" which the

Greenock *Advertiser* had already published the previous Friday, June 11. Much of the article has to do with the Presbyterian General Assembly's opposition to Rev. John McLeod Campbell, while the remainder is concerned with the reports of supernatural gifts, which reports were just starting to circulate. The scoffing reaction of most of the publications of the period can readily be seen in this article.

> . . . the public have already been made fully acquainted with the miracles of speaking in unknown tongues and writing in unknown languages—the miraculous healing of the sick, and the attempt to make the lame walk without crutches—and other affected doings, equally insane and ridiculous.—That these have been countenanced openly or tacitly, by the leading professors of certain opinions, there is scarcely room to doubt. . . .
>
> A contemporary journal published last Saturday a letter from an individual in Port-Glasgow, giving an account of a pretended case of miraculous healing. A manuscript copy of this precious epistle had been some weeks in our possession, and would have been presented to our readers, but for the restraint which we had imposed upon ourselves, as before noticed, and also because we were by no means anxious to be the first to give to the world so melancholy a record of perverted judgment and bad taste, amounting almost to profanity of language. But this is not the only *morceau* of the kind which has been handing about; a more important one, in many respects, is the letter of Miss Mary Campbell, of Fernicarry, whose gift of writing and speaking in unknown tongues has raised her so high in the estimation of the fanatics. It is true her miracle did not precede, but followed the other, and indeed appears to have arisen out of it, so that it wants the merit of originality . . .

There is no mention in this article of Margaret Macdonald or her views, only of Mary Campbell and her activities. It almost seems that spectacular Mary "stole the show" from stay-at-home Margaret, though probably not intentionally since both were close friends. The article does include a letter written by Mary to Rev. Campbell, in which she describes her healing and says "I received our dear brother's letter, giving me an account of his sister [Margaret Macdonald] having been raised up, and commanding me to rise up and walk," but the newspaper reporter mentions neither Margaret nor her brothers by name.

The Wednesday, June 2, 1830, Edinburgh *Scotsman* carried an article entitled "The Gareloch Miracles." Part of the account is an abridgment of a similar article on the manifestations, previously appearing in an issue of the Glasgow *Free Press*; their diatribe is followed by this paragraph written by the *Scotsman* reporter:

> The above is a short history of the commencement of the miracle-workers, but what will the end of these things be? One might suppose that the superior intelligence of even the lower population of Scotland would at once have buried these absurdities in ridicule and contempt. But no! even a clergyman has been sucked into the Gareloch whirlpool of blasphemy, and is preaching and teaching the new creed, and encouraging the working of miracles with all his might. Next we are told that a writer to the signet has given the right hand of fellowship to the presumptuous spinster of "the tongues"; and, (tell it not in Gath!) it is a fact that the wiseacres of Cambridge University have had their wits employed in decyphering the dark sayings of Miss Mary, and have absolutely pronounced the "new tongues" to *resemble* Chinese! Gramercy! if the Sublime Brother of the Moon hears this, we much fear he will come over and lay claim to these our poor dear kingdoms, and then woe unto schoolmasters and steam companies—they will be blown up for ever! We are the more alarmed on this point, because we believe no real miracle will ever be performed but through the agency of the schoolmaster and the steam-engine—at least until the dawn of the millenium—so we beg leave respectfully to decline believing in the Gareloch Infatuates, and recommend all our readers to do the same, aye and until the aforesaid agents are specially associated with every pretended miracle.

Boase records some of the contemptuous phrases various London publications employed in later days in their description of the charismatic gifts of the period. Some of these phrases, along with the corresponding publishers, included:

"blasphemous fooleries" (*Times*), "disgusting profanities" (*Morning Chronicle*), "wild delusions" (*Record*), "extravagancies" (*Christian Observer*), "monstrous folly" (*Christian Advocate*), and "infatuated talk" (*Evangelical Magazine*) . . .[4]

When John Darby of the Brethren heard about the unusual goings on in Scotland in the middle of 1830, he decided to investigate for himself.

The famous Fry Collection of early Brethren letters and papers, in the possession of C. E. Fry who lives on England's Isle of Wight, contains some helpful material verifying Darby's visit to western Scotland during the period in question.[5] But the best source of knowledge as to whether or not Darby went to Scotland is Darby himself. In his book *The Irrationalism of Infidelity* (1853), a reply to Francis William Newman's account in *Phases of Faith* (1850) of his own visit there, Darby discloses much valuable information in what he says—and especially in what he doesn't say! Darby's entire narrative of his visit is as follows:

But I must here (without any reproach to Mr. N. [F. W. Newman], as it is a matter of memory) recall some facts, and rectify some statements. At Pentecost the languages were universally understood by those who spoke them; the Irvingite tongues never by any one: a notable difference. And this is so true, that after first trying their hand at making Chinese of it, it was suggested among them that it might be the tongue of angels, as it was said, "Though I speak with the tongues of men and of angels"—delightful idea!

Mr. N. is not quite exact in his account of the report of the "Irish Clergyman," [6] or at least of what the "Irish Clergyman" saw and heard. There was a pretended interpretation. Two brothers (respectable shipbuilders at Port Glasgow, of the name of M'D——), and their sister [Margaret Macdonald], were the chief persons who spoke, with a Gaelic maid-servant, in the tongues, and a Mrs. J——, in English. J. M'D—— spoke, on the occasion alluded to, for about a quarter of an hour, with great energy and fluency, in a semi-Latin sounding speech—then sung a hymn in the same. Having finished, he knelt down and prayed there might be interpretation; as God had given one gift, that He would add the other. His sister got up at the opposite side of the room, and professed to give the interpretation; but it was a string of texts on overcoming, and no hymn, and one, if not more, of the texts was quoted wrongly. Just afterwards there was a bustle; and apparently some one was unwell, and went into the next room; and the gifted English-speaking person, with utterances from the highest pitch of voice to the lowest murmur, with all strange prolongation of tones, spoke through (if one may so express oneself), as if passing through, the agony of Christ. Once the Gaelic servant spoke briefly in "a tongue," not, if the "Irish Clergyman" remembers right, the same evening. The sense he had of the want of the power of the Holy Ghost in the Church made him willing to hear and see. Yet he went rather as deputed for others than for himself.

The excitement was great, so that, though not particularly an excitable person, he felt its effects very strongly. It did not certainly approve itself to his judgment; other things contributed to form it. It was too much of a scene. Previous to the time of exercising the gifts, they read, sung psalms, and prayed, under certain persons' presidence (one of them a very estimable person, whom he has since seen free from all this, and a minister of an independent or some dissenting church in Edinburgh, then a church-elder). This being finished, the "Irish Clergyman" was going away, when another said to him, "Don't go: the best part is probably to come yet." So he stayed, and heard what has just been related. He was courteously admitted, as one not believing, who came to see what was the real truth of the case. The parties are mostly dead, or dispersed, and many freed from the delusion, and the thing itself public; so that he does not feel he is guilty of any indiscretion in giving a correct account of what passed.

It may be added, without of course saying anything that could point out the persons, that female vanity, and very distinct worldliness, did not confirm, to his mind, the thought that it could be the Spirit's power. The M'D——s were, in ordinary life, quiet, sober men, and, he believes, most blameless. Their names were so public that there is no indelicacy in alluding to them;

but the "Irish Clergyman" did not think they had that kind of peace and deliverance from legal thoughts, which is a sign in another way of the Spirit's power. They never received the apostolic pretensions of London and Albury, but repudiated, in the strongest way and on full enquiry, the blasphemous doctrine of the Irvingites as to the person of the Lord. Mr. N.'s reporter, the "Irish Clergyman," doubts that they were in the least aware of it at the time they professed to receive the gifts; but they certainly entirely repudiated it when he saw them afterwards.[7]

It's incredible that Darby could remember such small details and even quote words uttered in the Macdonald home after twenty-three years, and yet be silent on the central theme of the manifestations—Margaret's pre-trib rapture teaching! He says that he "came to see what was the real truth of the case," but on this he is silent. And he adds that he is "giving a correct account of what passed," but just how correct is it if such a significant aspect is carefully avoided? [8]

When Darby wrote this book in 1853 he could knowingly say "the parties are mostly dead, or dispersed," for he had preserved an understandably special interest in the young and unassuming Scottish lassie from whom he had borrowed a key ingredient for his dispensational system of prophetic interpretation! True, Margaret saw a series of raptures (and she was actually a partial rapturist, with or without the label), but we must remember that the first of her raptures was indeed a pre-trib translation which would remove some of the believers from the earth before the Antichrist was to be revealed. Darby borrowed from her, modified her views, and then popularized them under his own name without giving her credit. (Sandeen's *The Roots of Fundamentalism* points out that Darby was intolerant of other prophetic teachers.) Darby, then, did his part to draw attention away from the *real* origin of his special teaching.

Let's look now at another early writer who also made an important contribution—Robert Baxter of Doncaster, England. His book, *Narrative of Facts, Characterizing the Supernatural Manifestations in Members of Mr. Irving's Con-*

gregation, and Other Individuals, in England and Scotland, and Formerly in the Writer Himself was published in 1833. Baxter had gone down to London in the fall of 1831, visited some of the prayer meetings which preceded the manifestations in Irving's church, and soon was a regular attendant at Irving's services. He then became endowed with the prophetic utterances and had a number of personal revelations. Later, when certain prophecies made by him and others simply were not fulfilled, he became disillusioned and felt that he had been deceived and had in turn deceived others.

He refers in places to the Port Glasgow incidents, the taking up of pre-trib teaching by Irving, and the later effects of such doctrine. In the first part of his book he says:

> . . . I had heard many particulars of the extraordinary manifestations which had occurred at Port Glasgow, in Scotland. A near relation of mine, having a friend, a clergyman of the Church of England, residing in the neighbourhood; I had, from time to time, received accounts through him, of what was going on there.[9]

Several pages later Baxter has a fascinating paragraph which, amazingly enough, contains three Bible passages that are also found *in the same sequence* in Margaret's pre-trib revelation! He writes:

> An opinion had been advanced in some of Mr. Irving's writings, that before the second coming of Christ, and before the setting in upon the world of the *day of vengeance*, emphatically so called in the Scriptures, the saints would be caught up to heaven like Enoch and Elijah; and would be thus saved from the destruction of this world, as Noah was saved in the ark, and as Lot was saved from Sodom. This was an opinion I never could entertain; conceiving, as I did, that our refuge in and through the days of vengeance, would be some earthly sanctuary, until the Lord should come, the dead be raised, and those remaining alive should be caught up. (I Thess. iv. 17.) In the interval I have alluded to I did, however, experience a sudden change of opinion[10]; the passages in Matt. xxiv. *Two shall be in the field, one*

shall be taken, and the other left; two women shall be grinding at the mill, the one shall be taken, and the other left, were brought to me in the power, accompanied with the sudden conviction I have before described—"This is the translation of the saints, whilst the rest of the world are left in their usual occupations." Another passage was also brought to me—Luke xxi. 36. *Watch ye, therefore, and pray always, that ye may be accounted worthy to escape all these things that shall come to pass, and to stand before the Son of Man,"*—accompanied by the same overpowering conviction, "This escape is from the days of vengeance, and the standing before the Son, is for those who are counted worthy to be translated." I was from this time fully convinced that there would be a translation of the saints, and my conviction was confirmed in a most remarkable manner. My wife, though agreeing with me in general, on doctrine and in faith, was never able to believe in the utterance and power as of God; but considered it to be a deceit of Satan, and was most violently opposed to it, and all views connected with it. About a fortnight after my conviction, concerning the translation of the saints, I was casually mentioning my view to a friend who called, when my wife started, and said, "Why, have you changed your opinion?" I had, for some time past, avoided any allusion to these subjects before her; but on mutual explanation, I found the same change, unknown to me, had taken place in her view; and, at the same time the conviction was brought to me by the texts of Scripture, a like conviction was brought to her in the form of a revelation, as though a voice had said to her, "The ark is prepared in the heavens, wait for it;" her mind carried, at the same moment, into the troubles coming upon the world, and receiving the assurance of safety in heaven. This was the more remarkable, as she did not believe in such revelations, or in the work; and though she was convinced of this as a revelation, yet it did not bring her to believe that the power of utterance or other manifestations were of God.[11]

Baxter also speaks of various revelations he experienced at one time or another. One concerned both a *mystical* man of sin in II Thessalonians and the Holy Spirit:

The *mystical* man of sin, (2 Thess. iii.) was also explained to be the spirit of Satan, the prince of this world, now bearing rule in the visible church; manifest by the worldly mindedness found in her, and to be (as it was declared) yet more manifest in the opposition she would give to the work and power of the Spirit, as God would shortly pour down his Spirit and shew forth his power—that when the Spirit of God was withdrawn from the visible church, the spirit of Satan entered in and bore sway—and that this was what was contained in 2 Thess. ii. 6, *And now ye know what withholdeth that he might be revealed in his time. For the mystery of iniquity doth already work, only he who now letteth will let, until he be taken out of the way, and then shall that wicked be revealed*—as above, ver. 4: *Sitting in the temple of God, shewing himself that he is God. He who letteth* was declared to be the Spirit of God; and the taking of this let out of the way, to be the taking away of the Spirit of God from the visible church.[12]

He saw a distinction between a *mystical* man of sin and the Antichrist. Of the latter he writes:

The person who should be so energized of Satan, and be set up as his Christ, was at a subsequent period, declared to be young Napoleon.[13]

One of Baxter's many revelations had to do with America:

A prophecy, the details of which occurred on several days, during this visit to London, must not be forgotten. One evening, at Mr. P.'s, I met Mr. R. who had come from North America, and had been a missionary among the Indians there.—I had in the country received an utterance and revelation concerning America, which I was mentioning, when he declared his opinion, that the American Indians were the lost ten tribes of Israel. He asked me, if I had any teaching upon it. I told him I had not, and after hearing from him that one of their native chiefs was converted, and now in London, I thought no more of it. A few mornings afterwards, at breakfast at Mr. Irving's, a conversation arose upon America, and I mentioned what had been revealed to me concerning it; and Mr. Irving asked, with reference to some utterance, whether I should conclude it referred to the ten tribes. I paused, for the power rested upon me, and after a little time, it was distinctly revealed in the power, and I was made to utter that the American Indians were the lost ten tribes. . . .[14]

Baxter had become interested in the charismatic revival in 1831. By 1833, when his book was published, he was completely convinced that the Irvingite movement in London was not of God. Among other things he talks about the fact of secrecy respecting their doctrines:

> There are some general characteristics in the work, which, apart from doctrines or instances of failure of predictions, cast suspicion upon it. One is the extreme secrecy enjoined by the spirit, and the manifest shrinking from public examination. The spirit has, both in England and Scotland, forbidden the writing down of utterances, and even the attempt to repeat them verbatim. Thus errors and contradictions are more easily concealed and explained away.[15]

Towards the end of the book Baxter writes:

> In conclusion, I cannot refrain from adding a remark or two upon the causes which have, as it appears to me, prepared the way for this awful delusion. . . . In the front I would place a habit of speculating upon religious truths, in the hasty interpretation of Scripture, and especially the prophetic portions. . . . Surely we have so much of glorious revelation made plain to us, that we can feed upon it in peace and patience, with thanksgiving; and need not to cultivate an unhealthy appetite after crude and novel views, in which we can neither find rest nor edification. Our minds are naturally prone to novelty, and vain curiosity is one of the strongest of our temptations.[16]

Though not mentioning the Macdonalds by name, Baxter points briefly to the gifted persons at Port Glasgow.

> It is well known, that the delusion first appeared in Scotland, and it was brought to London by Mrs. C. [Mrs. John Cardale], who was one of the speakers, and gifted at Port Glasgow. There, as far as I am informed, it has made little progress; and it was not until adopted and upheld by Mr. Irving, that it began to challenge much attention, and extend its influence. No doubt many persons, warmly attached to Mr. Irving, upheld his general doctrines, and so sustained the heresy, though they did not themselves fully embrace it: this was the case, both with my

brother and myself, and we neither of us knew what were really
the doctrines held by him until, by the course I have mentioned,
we were brought to examine them; and, at the same time, to
separate from them. . . .

One circumstance of these manifestations cannot but force
itself upon observation; that is, the continual use which was
made of the doctrine of the second advent of our Lord. This was
the leading theme of the utterances. The nearness of it, its
suddenness, and the fearful judgments which would accompany
it, were the continual arguments which were used to excite our
minds, and stimulate our decision; as well as to support us under
difficulties, and to induce us to lay all other things aside to
further the work. . . .

. . . there must have been much error, in our view of the
manner and circumstances of the coming of the Lord, or we
could not have been so deceived.[17]

How strange, how *unbelievable* that the pre-trib view
should have such a hidden background for such a length of
time! A second look at the development of prophecy in the
1830s makes one realize that many crucial details concerning
the formulation of beliefs in that period have largely been
hidden from view. The current freedom, and willingness, to
take such a second look was exhibited in an editorial in the
July, 1972, issue of a British evangelical magazine, *The
Witness*, which said in part:

What strikes us as amazing is the swiftness in which doctrines
unknown previous to Darby became so widely accepted as to be
regarded as almost fundamental to the Christian faith. Without
doubt from the first there were many men of influence who
differed from Darby. We have only to mention B. W. Newton, or
Robert Chapman, to show that other views on prophecy were
held by many. Had it not been for the dominant personality of
Darby and his gifts as a teacher, other views would have gone
alongside Darby's view from the first, and there would have been
less intolerance of views differing from those he popularized.
Even Darby himself hesitated at the first before swallowing the
view he afterwards held so tenaciously concerning the Gospel by
Matthew as being Jewish and dispensational in character. It is

fortunate that nowadays an evergrowing number of thinkers amongst Brethren are free to hold their views without a heresy-hunt, on this and other matters of a non-fundamental character.[18]

NOTES

1. P. 1.
2. It is quite possible Margaret was still living when Norton first published her pre-trib revelation in his 1840 *Memoirs*, reason enough for him to accommodate the publicity-shunning Macdonalds by not revealing her at that time as the pre-trib originator.
3. *The Catholic Apostolic Church*, pp. 1–2.
4. *Supplementary Narrative*, p. 787.
5. Harold Rowdon's *The Origins of the Brethren* (1967) and F. Roy Coad's *A History of the Brethren Movement* (1968) are two works including much data from this valuable source. I am grateful to C. E. Fry, for sharing one of Newton's early letters in which he wrote that Darby "stayed a fortnight or three weeks" as an observer in Mary Campbell's home after learning she had "spirit gifts." Darby left after deciding that "the work was not of God." Fry could find no mention of Margaret Macdonald in his collection, although there are numerous references to Irvingism.
6. The title Newman gave Darby in *Phases of Faith*, p. 27.
7. Pp. 283–285.
8. For an astounding summary of documentation from various sources, including other Brethren, relative to unreliability and untruthfulness in Darby's narratives, see Rowdon's *The Origins of the Brethren*, pp. 252–253, footnote 7.
9. P. 3.
10. At this point he suddenly changed his mind. On January 14, 1832, Baxter had a revelation that believers would be caught up after the last 1260 days of what he then thought was the great tribulation, and he set a date—July 14, 1835.
11. Pp. 17–18.
12. Pp. 29–30. In *The Rapture—When?*, p. 14, Wheaton College professor Arthur Katterjohn says that in II Thess. 2:7 "there is no word for 'taken' in the Greek, nor any thought of 'taken' implied. This was added by the translators." On the next page he adds that II Thess. 2:7b should read "until he become (or arise) out of the midst." In other words, says Katterjohn, God will continue to let (hinder or restrain) until he (Antichrist) be (become or arise) out of the way (midst).

13. P. 31.
14. P. 80. An apparent tie-in with this is found in a footnote in Edward
    Miller's *The History and Doctrines of Irvingism* (1878), Vol. II, p. 200:
    "Though as a matter of fact there was a leakage from Irvingism to
    Mormonism. One of the Members of the former Body left it, and
    brought with him to the then nascent Mormonism several Tenets and
    points of organization which he had learnt amongst his first friends."
15. P. 126.
16. Pp. 138–139.
17. Pp. 141–143.
18. I am grateful to G. C. D. Howley, editor of *The Witness* for many
    years, for permission to quote from "A Short-Lived Journal," which
    discussed William Kelly's *The Prospect. The Witness* originated among
    Brethren and is the oldest-circulating magazine among them.

10. BOILING IT DOWN

We have seen that a young Scottish lassie named Margaret Macdonald had a private revelation in Port Glasgow, Scotland, in the early part of 1830 that a select group of Christians would be caught up to meet Christ in the air *before* the days of Antichrist. An eye-and-ear-witness, Robert Norton M.D., preserved her handwritten account of her pre-trib rapture revelation in two of his books, and said it was the *first* time anyone ever split the second coming into two distinct parts, or stages. His writings, along with much other Catholic Apostolic Church literature, have been hidden many decades from the mainstream of evangelical thought and only recently have surfaced.

Margaret's views were well-known to those who visited her home, among them John Darby of the Brethren. Within a few months her distinctive prophetic outlook was mirrored in the September, 1830, issue of *The Morning Watch* and the early Brethren assembly at Plymouth, England. Early disciples of the pre-trib interpretation often called it a new doctrine.[1] Setting dates for Christ's return was a common practice at that time.[2]

Divisiveness and rivalry among different denominations kept valuable knowledge hidden which would have benefited everyone. (This continuing spirit of division seriously hampers a united effort today on the part of all true believers to reach for Christ an almost completely heathen world!)

Following my discovery of Norton's book in an Illinois

bookstore in 1971, and before our trip to Great Britain, I corresponded with a number of top scholars, sharing excerpts from the book and asking their reactions. (These men are evangelical leaders and their names are as familiar to Christians as Coca-Cola is around the globe.)

A Missouri seminary president wrote back: "It really is a most interesting historical fact to observe that the pre-tribulation rapture originated in this astonishing way."

A professor in a Texas seminary said in a letter: "What is stated in Norton's book is new to me, and I am unable to evaluate it. My understanding was that, while Darby was the main spokesman for pre-tribulationism, there were many with whom he was associated that were studying together and developed this doctrine almost simultaneously."

An Oregon Bible teacher wrote: "You will be interested to know that many years ago I had dinner in Seattle with a then middle-aged couple who were members of the Catholic Apostolic Church (Irvingite sect). At that time I believed in pre-tribism and told them so. They asked me where I got the doctrine. I told them 'from the Bible'. They said, 'No, you didn't' and went on to tell me how it was not in the Bible but revealed to their church through one of their prophetesses around the middle of the 19th century."

A Kentucky seminary professor who is also a noted author said this in reply: "On biblical and historical grounds I had traced the idea of a pre-tribulation rapture to J. N. Darby about the year 1830, but I did not know about Margaret McDonald. Thanks so very much for helping me on this point. It is good to have theological detectives of your type who will trace things down."

A Minnesota college professor and well-known authority on dispensational development wrote: "Let me say, first of all, that I should be most grateful to you if you would send me the complete photostat of Miss M. M.'s remarks. The photostat you sent ended at the bottom of page 15 of Norton's book before M. M. had actually said anything about the any-moment coming. The photographed passage contains only Norton's statement that Miss M. M. had revealed the doctrine of the two comings. I presume that she does say something more explicit in the following pages of her transcribed testimony. If she does, I would be most interested in seeing it. Whenever I have traced down references to the origin of the doctrine of the any-moment coming in an ecstatic utterance in Irving's church, I have run into this same problem. The utterance which is supposed to contain the revelation in fact contains nothing of substance. If Miss M. M.'s testimony does in fact contain a clear statement of the doctrine I would be most interested to see it."

A foremost evangelical scholar in England wrote that "any further information that you may bring to light about the question will be widely welcomed."

These replies are representative of those from hundreds of scholars, and the really big surprise was to discover that the overwhelming majority of today's best-known evangelical scholars has rejected the idea of a secret two-stage rapture even though these same scholars have largely been in the dark about the origin of such teaching.[3]

In the preceding pages are many references to speaking in unknown tongues. The evidence I have been privileged to find has shown that Margaret had her pre-trib revelation *before* she ever spoke with tongues; in fact, the tongues were a completely separate item (although some early pre-trib teachers were indeed tongues-speakers) and pre-trib rapture doctrine did not originate in an utterance of tongues, as some have charged. Margaret claimed her revelation was based only upon her study of Scripture passages.

Concerning charismatic gifts as they appear in various denominations today, since the overwhelming majority of present-day Bible scholars of note sees but a single unified coming of Christ for His church *after* the days of Antichrist, which are days "such as hath not been from the beginning of the world until now, no, nor ever shall be" (Matt. 24:21, ASV), it is possible that the Holy Spirit will empower the church during those days in ways we know little or nothing about right now.

In light of the evidence I have prayerfully and carefully given in this book relative to the pre-trib origin (which origin has been hidden for a long time), I would ask all Bible teachers to declare a moratorium on such teaching, at least until they can check this out for themselves.

This, then, is the true story of the unbelievable pre-trib origin.

NOTES

1. One of the earliest Brethren leaders, Robert Gribble, described in Rowdon's *The Origins of the Brethren*, p. 152, as one who "has been strangely neglected in most works on Brethren history," confessed in the early 1830s, after becoming acquainted with other Brethren, that he had adopted "a new view of unfulfilled prophecy" (Rowdon's book, p. 149) which included a pre-trib return of Christ. In an unguarded letter to a friend on July 24, 1834 (*Letters of J.N.D.*, pp. 25–26), Darby advocated a subtle introduction of the new pre-trib rapture view: "I think we ought to have something more of direct testimony as to the Lord's coming, and its bearing also on the state of the church: ordinarily, it would not be well to have it so clear, as it frightens people. We must pursue it steadily; it works like leaven, and its fruit is by no means seen yet; I do not mean leaven as ill, but the thoughts are new, and people's minds work on them, and all the old habits are against their feelings . . . ." Note again Darby's admission that "the thoughts are new"—not "rediscovered"! Those who espouse the pre-trib view cannot name even one person from the time of Christ until 1830 who ever taught such a doctrine.

2. Darby himself was a date-setter at one time. In his *Etudes sur l'Epitre aux Hebreux*, published in Lausanne, Switzerland, about 1835, he writes on p. 146: "There are excellent brethren in all countries who have sought to calculate these dates . . . some have fixed 1844, others 1847; I myself have made several calculations in the times past, and in the same sense."

3. For a free copy of this survey of hundreds of scholars entitled "A Long

List of Post-Tribs," on may write to: Heart of America Bible Society, Box 420, Liberty, Missouri 04068.

4. An outstanding book that I would recommend is entitled *Christians Will Go Through The Tribulation — And How To Prepare For It*. This book has a vital message for Christians today. It can be ordered from Omega Publications at P.O. Box 4130, Medford, Oregon 97501. (You can use the order form at the back of this book.)

PART II
The Late Great Pre-Trib Rapture

11. A FEW SHOCKS

The other day I opened up a newspaper with these alarming headlines:

MILLIONS MISSING AROUND WORLD
MASS KIDNAPPING
STOCK MARKET FACES CRASH
THOUSANDS ATTEMPT SUICIDE

The articles in the tabloid-size paper described scenes of horror and anguish around the globe—planes crashing, killer earthquakes, volcanoes erupting and tidal waves raging, teenage terror mobs roaming city streets, thousands of persons dying of heart attacks, and so on.

But my only response was a hearty chuckle. Why? Because this paper was merely another attempt to portray what many persons believe will happen when Christ returns for His church. They are the modern proponents of the pre-tribulation rapture, or pre-trib rapture—the sudden, unannounced happening that will cause the immediate disappearance of millions of true Christians from every nation. This same attitude is even expressed on bumper stickers like the one that warns: IF DRIVER DISAPPEARS, GRAB THE WHEEL.

We've already examined the bizarre origin of this doctrine and the apparent attempt to conceal it by J. N. Darby. Now I want to evaluate its widespread effects in western Christendom, especially in America. Beyond that I want to advocate a return to the more realistic post tribulational view, which was the only option within premillennialism prior to 1830 and which today is still the view held by the majority of premillennial Bible scholars. Christ's coming to receive His church and to judge the world will be one event, not two.

True, there are some scholars who affirm this but have not called themselves post-tribs, and in some cases their idea of the great tribulation has differed from the concepts of a seven or a three-and-a-half-year period.

But all have believed in a single coming of the Lord in the future, with the "catching up" of I Thessalonians 4 taking place *after* the days of Antichrist. Post-mills and a-mills, of course, hold to a single coming of Christ and *most* pre-mills, believe it or not, also see a one-stage advent that is necessarily post-tribulational.

There are at least two reasons why many Christians, especially here in America, are unaware that most of the top biblical scholars in the world today are post-tribs: (1) post-trib silence and (2) the vociferous dissemination of pre-trib ideas by their advocates.

The Silent Majority

George Ladd, a well-known post-trib pre-mill professor at Fuller Theological Seminary, stated in *The Blessed Hope*, p. 159, that those who see the church on earth during the days of Antichrist include a significant number of Christian leaders, but he added that they haven't been vocal, haven't wanted to be quoted, and haven't publicly declared their prophetic position.

One good reason for this silence is the fact that pre-trib dispensationalists have often used any and all means to quash their opposition, examples of which will be given in later pages.

Harry Conn, president of Men For Missions in Minneapolis, told me in a letter: "In my estimation dispensational truth is a cacophony of hermeneutical mendacity, and any kindly disagreement with it is usually answered by a meaningless riposte."

The Pre-Trib Rapture view has caused the deaths of thousands of persons. Veteran missionary H. A. Baker shares his experiences of thirty-four years on the mission field in China in several of his books, including *Through Tribulation, Tribulation to Glory, Visions Beyond the Veil,* and *God in Ka Do Land.* He graphically points out the link between beliefs and actions.

Baker and other post-trib missionaries warned many Chinese Christians that Antichrist would come before Christ returns. Many heeded the warning and, before the Communist takeover, fled to the mountains where they have been able to continue witnessing for many years.

On the other hand, many pre-trib missionaries assured believers that they would be raptured away *before* any time of persecution—and history tells us that tens of thousands of Chinese Christians have been murdered since 1949!

In his book *Re-entry*, p. 124, John Wesley White quotes *Time* magazine as reporting that tens of thousands of Christians are now languishing in prisons in China and Russia and other Communist countries. Those believers are, in some cases, undergoing torture, and their children are taken from them if they teach them about Christ.

Corrie ten Boom has also spoken of the Chinese Christians and their suffering: "the Christians were told that they didn't have to go through tribulation and we all know how it is in China." She added that all other Christians in free lands better be prepared for what is coming to them also. And in her article "The Coming Tribulation" in the Nov.–Dec., 1974 *Logos Journal* she wrote that those teaching "there will be no tribulation" and "the Christians will be able to escape all this" are really "the false teachers Jesus was warning us to expect in the latter days."

In *Sodom Had No Bible*, p. 94, British evangelist Leonard

Ravenhill also emphasizes that God didn't provide a rapture in 1940 for the Chinese Christians, nor for the believers in Hungary or in Russia.

Demos Shakarian, director of the Full Gospel Businessmen, says that the Holy Spirit is now being poured out on believers to prepare them for rough times ahead. And Richard Wurmbrand told me that believers in Russia describe their existence these days as one of great tribulation and suffering. He added that America and other western countries will have the same thing one of these days. Larry Norman's song, "Right Here in America," also warns of persecution heading our way.

Louis Berkhof, writing as an a-mill, says in his book *The Second Coming of Christ*, pp. 24–5, that though there have been signs of apostasy and tribulation down through the centuries, their final form apparently hasn't appeared yet. He then quotes Matthew 24:21–22: "For then shall be great tribulation, such as was not since the beginning of the world to this time, no, nor ever shall be. And except those days should be shortened, there should no flesh be saved: but for the elect's sake those days shall be shortened."

Things to Come

In the following pages I intend to share many aspects and effects of pre-trib rapture teaching. You'll hear about a good number of Christian leaders who are post-trib, and you'll also be informed of some outstanding pre-trib leaders. You'll learn that the majority of well-known Jewish believers of the last century (the first century of pre-tribism) was strongly post-trib.

You'll find out how pre-trib teaching has influenced evangelism and missions, and discover that students at key pre-trib schools are turning back to the historic post-trib view in rapidly increasing numbers—often without school authorities knowing about it! You'll gain knowledge of the ways in which pre-trib has stayed in power so long and you'll also be given a long second look at Hal Lindsey's popular book *The Late Great Planet Earth* and some of his other writings.

Before you've reached the last page, you'll probably agree that the pre-trib rapture view is on its last legs—if it ever had a leg to stand on!

12. PRE VERSUS POST

Most of the current hyperventilation over the church-in-the-trib issue seems to involve the spokesmen for the pre-trib and post-trib camps. Thus I will briefly outline the major points in the pre-trib theory and compare them with corresponding answers from the post-tribs.

Who Are the Elect?

Matt. 24:21–22 establishes that the days of the tribulation will be shortened for the sake of His elect. Pre-tribs say that the elect in this passage are Israel and not the church. Post-tribs maintain that all saints, whether Jew or Gentile, are in view simply because in this chapter there is no hint of rapture before the coming of Christ in glory at the end of the tribulation.

Pre-tribs admit that the great commission in Matthew 28:19–20 should be carried out by the church, but then turn around and claim that Matthew, Mark, and Luke are on "Jewish" ground. If this is true, why do the first three gospels record the ministry in Galilee of the Gentiles? And why does John, who, everyone agrees, is on "church" ground, contain the *Jerusalem* ministry?

The Rapture Passage

One of the passages used most frequently to teach a pre-trib rapture is I Thessalonians 4:13–18. Radio preachers and others constantly recite these verses as if repetition can bring about the miracle of a translation of saints *before* the tribulation. Instead of calling this the rapture passage, we should call it the resurrection passage; the dead in Christ are clearly in view in the first five verses and implied in the last verse, but the "catching up" is mentioned only once—in verse 17.

It's unfortunate that there is a chapter division right after I Thessalonians 4:18. I Thessalonians 5:1 begins with the word "But" (a connecting word). Anyone reading both chapters without interruption can easily see that chapter five continues to describe I Thessalonians 4:13–18 as the "day of the Lord"—the time when "sudden destruction" comes on the ungodly world. This ties in with the coming of Christ in judgment. All of which means that the church's "catching up" will be post-trib; if sudden destruction were to take place *before* or *during* the tribulation, how could there be a tribulation? (Scofield's notes even refer I Thessalonians 5 to the day of Jehovah—which is in a post-trib setting!)

Moreover, the word "Lord" is found five times in I Thessalonians 4:13–18, which supposedly describes the "day of Christ." And "Christ" is mentioned only *once*. Is the "day of Christ" supposed to be distinguished from the "day of the Lord"? Do these terms denote, as pre-tribs insist they do, *two different stages* of the second coming? If so, then there must be at least twenty-one different stages because at least twenty-one different terms are found in the Bible that refer to the second advent.

Imminence

Walvoord's *The Rapture Question*, pp. 53–55, states that the doctrine of imminency is the heart and central feature of pretribulationism. Theodore Epp declared on his *Back to the Bible* broadcast that he knew of no greater incentive for holy living than the "any-moment" return of Christ for His own. This, however, overlooks the immediate involvement of the

Holy Spirit in each of our lives. His judgments and superintendence should motivate us to holy living as surely as anything. We love Jesus because He first loved us, and our love for Him shouldn't be any less intense even if He isn't coming back for a thousand years.

Pre-tribs tell us that we can't look for Christ's imminent return because certain things have to happen *first.* Thus the rapture is imminent, but the second coming is not.

II Peter 3:12–13 reminds us to be looking for the time when "elements shall melt with fervent heat" and looking for "new heavens and a new earth"—all of which is at least a thousand years away, according to many pre-tribs. Why, then, can't we watch for a post-trib coming that might be just a few years away?

It's fantastic how two-stagers can strain at a seven-year "gnat" but swallow a thousand-year "camel."

It's also amazing that, in the pre-trib scheme of things, the tribulation saints *can* watch (see the "watch" verses in Matthew 24 and 25) for a second coming that follows intervening events—the very same coming pre-tribs say the church could never look for.

Non-Imminent Arguments

Here are a few succinct reasons for rejecting any-moment doctrine, especially if one sees a *future* Antichrist; most of these points are developed at length in my father's book *Triumph Through Tribulation:*

1. Great Commission fulfillment implies a long period of time.
2. Seed growth in Matthew 13 is a time-consuming process.
3. Paul expected death, not rapture, in II Timothy 4:6–8.
4. Jesus predicted Peter's martyrdom in John 21:18–19.
5. Matthew 24 teaches that signs must come first.
6. Many passages speak of a large interval between Christ's ascension and return: Jewish dispersion into "all na-

tions" (Luke 21); "man travelling into a *far* country," "after a *long time* the lord of those servants cometh" (Matthew 25).

7. Apostasy of last days takes time to develop.
8. Bridegroom tarried in parable of virgins.
9. Pastoral epistles teach Church's continuing ministry, which involves time.
10. Paul says Christ's coming is *not* imminent (II Thessalonians 2:1–3), for apostasy and Antichrist must come *first.*
11. View of seven phases of church history (seven churches of Revelation) involves big lapse of time and imminence difficulties for pre-tribs; could Christ have come before the last phase?
12. Exhortations to watch and be ready are tied to what pre-trib teachers regard as the *second stage* in Matthew 24 and 25, I Corinthians 1:7, Colossians 3:4, I Thessalonians 3:13, II Thessalonians 1:7–10, I Peter 1:13, and 4:13, and I John 2:28.

Wrongly Dividing

Pre-tribbers love to quote from the second century work known as the *Didache* (and the section entitled "The teaching of the Twelve Apostles") to prove that the early Church believed in imminency. The *Didache* (II, 16) reads: "Watch for your life's sake. Let not your lamps be quenched, nor your loins unloosed; but be ye ready, for ye know not the hour in which our Lord cometh."

Robert H. Gundry's new book *The Church and the Tribulation,* p. 175, quotes these lines from the *Didache* which at first glance *do* seem to teach an imminent coming. Right after this quote, however, post-tribber Gundry discloses in brackets that John F. Walvoord, Gerald B. Stanton, and J. Dwight Pentecost (in *Bibliotheca Sacra, Kept from the Hour,* and *Things to Come,* respectively) all omit to quote the rest of chapter sixteen which teaches the post-trib view and *not* imminence:

. . . for the whole time of your faith will not profit you, if ye be not made perfect in the last time. . . . Then shall appear the world-deceiver as Son of God, and shall do signs and wonders. . . . Then shall the creation of men come into the fire of trial, and many shall be made to stumble and perish; but they that endure in their faith shall be saved from under the curse itself.

Sometimes a pre-trib teacher, when asked to name anyone between the first century and 1830 who ever held to a pre-trib rapture, will answer something like this: "Well, you know, there were always those who believed the Lord could come at any moment." True, but *all* Christians before 1830 who held to an imminent coming really held to an imminent *post-trib* coming; they were convinced, during times of persecution, that they were probably *in* the tribulation and that some earthly ruler was the anticipated Antichrist. No one before 1830 ever believed in an imminent *pre-trib* coming. Nor did they differentiate the return of Christ and the rapture of the church.

Groups of Wrath

Pre-tribs teach that the church will never experience God's wrath (post-tribs heartily agree) and quote verses like John 5:24, Romans 5:9 and 8:1, I Thessalonians 1:10 and 5:9 to try to prove the church's exemption from the tribulation.

Do these verses *really* teach a pre-trib escape?

John 5:24 speaks of the "condemnation" that never comes to one who passes "from death unto life."

Romans 5:9 tells of being "saved from wrath"—the wrath that one escapes when he or she is "justified by his blood."

Romans 8:1 assures those "in Christ Jesus, who walk not after the flesh, but after the Spirit" that they are no longer under "condemnation."

I Thessalonians 1:10 refers to "Jesus, which delivered us from the wrath to come." Any wrath from which Jesus delivers, such as second coming wrath on the ungodly or eternal wrath of Hell, is not the Satanic wrath which gives the Tribulation its bad reputation. Even tribulation saints in the middle of persecution can stand on this verse and rest assured that a much greater wrath will eventually overtake their persecutors—a wrath that *no one* can withstand.

I Thessalonians 5:9 says that "God hath not appointed us to wrath, but to obtain salvation by our Lord Jesus Christ." If I wanted to reverse this text, I could say that Satan hasn't appointed us to salvation, but to obtain wrath. The opposite of salvation is not merely a time of tribulational testing, but the eternal wrath of God.

Even E. Schuyler English in his pre-trib book *Re-Thinking the Rapture*, pp. 56–7, admits that the last clause of I Thessalonians 1:10 is better rendered "who is delivering us from the wrath to come." He adds that this verse doesn't prove the pre-trib view. Most pre-trib leaders *do* know the difference between Satanic and godly wrath. But if their followers don't, they can easily be convinced of a pre-trib rapture with verses like I Thessalonians 1:10. If the tribulation is primarily Satanic wrath (from which no believer is ever immune), pre-trib promoters can best succeed in getting followers by giving the false impression that all tribulational wrath is *divine* wrath. Indeed, in *The Rapture Question* (billed as a "comprehensive" biblical study) Walvoord omits any mention of Revelation 12:12 which says "the *devil* is come down unto you, having great wrath. . . ."

Even if all tribulation wrath were exclusively divine wrath (which it isn't), God would have no more difficulty in distinguishing between the bad guys and the good guys than He had when He visited Egypt with plagues.

Actually, divine wrath commences only at *the very end* of the tribulation, and Ladd, Payne, Gundry and other post-trib authors carefully prove this point in their writings. Moreover, Payne's *The Imminent Appearing of Christ*, p. 172, contains a chart showing that all of the trumpet and bowl judgments (which mark the commencement of God's wrath) immediately preceding the appearing of Christ could happen in as little as fifteen minutes. And these judgments are directed only towards the ungodly—never at God's holy people.

A Literal Puzzle

Walvoord (*The Rapture Question*, pp. 56–7) maintains that pre-tribs interpret Scripture literally while post-tribs tend to spiritualize certain passages. But noted pre-tribbers such as Walter Scott, A. C. Gaebelein, and Harry A. Ironside say in their commentaries on the book of Revelation that the stars falling from heaven in chapter six are not to be taken literally but signify the downfall of certain leaders. Lindsey's *There's a New World Coming*, p. 110, sees in the stars Russian missiles streaking to earth.

On the other hand, post-trib commentators such as J. Barton Payne, S. I. McMillen, and Robert H. Gundry see no reason to spiritualize this passage. Gundry's *The Church and the Tribulation*, pp. 51–2, amply demonstrates that post-tribs can surpass pre-tribs in being literal minded.

Different Programs?

I Corinthians 10:32 mentions Jews, Gentiles, and the church. But do such verses require separate programs and the church's absence from the tribulation? Are pre-trib distinctions supported by Scripture?

Walvoord (*The Rapture Question*, p. 148) states that one's doctrine of the church determines whether or not the church will pass through the tribulation. On p. 16 he says that the doctrine of the church determines this whole question *more than passages dealing with the end times.*

Payne (*The Imminent Appearing of Christ*, pp. 124–5) contradicts Walvoord, saying that students should go over end-time passages *first* and then recheck their definition of the church if there is a conflict.

Are the church and Israel completely different, as pre-tribs claim? They say that, since the church is a "heavenly" body and Israel is an "earthly" one, the church will not be on earth during the tribulation.

The Bible, however, says that the Old Testament saints also had a heavenly hope (see Psalm 49:15, Hebrews 11:13–16) and that the church also has an earthly hope (see Revelation 2:26, 20:6, 21:1). The Old Testament saints were also born again and indwelt by the Holy Spirit (Ezekiel 36:26–7), as is the church. Is the church a bride? So was Israel in Hosea 2:20, 3:1–3. Was Israel a wife? So is the church in Revelation 19:7. Both Old and New Testament saints have found salvation through Christ (Hebrews 9:15), Moses was part of the "church" in the wilderness (Acts 7:37–8), and the church is described as "Abraham's seed" (Galatians 3:29), "the Israel of God" (Galatians 6:16), and "the commonwealth of Israel" (Ephesians 2:12).

Pre-tribs admit that the Spirit's outpouring prophesied in Joel 2:28–32 was at least partially fulfilled for the *church* in Acts 2:16–21, even though Joel didn't use the word "church" or any equivalent. They also admit that the new covenant foretold in Jeremiah 31:31–4 was fulfilled for the *church* in Hebrews 8:7–13, even though this prophecy was given to "the house of Israel" and "the house of Judah." (See Payne's above-mentioned book, pp. 123–33, for further similarities between the church and Israel.)

Are the church and tribulation saints distinctively different, as pre-tribs claim?

Both the church and tribulation saints are an earthly people (II Corinthians 5:1,4, Revelation 18:24). Both are world-wide (Galatians 3:8–9, Revelation 7:9). Both are also a heavenly people (Philippians 3:20, Revelation 7:15–7). Both are saved by grace and the blood of Christ (Ephesians 1:7, Revelation 7:14). Both are empowered by the Holy Spirit (Acts 1:8, I Corinthians 12:3, Mark 13:11). Both observe God's commandments and retain the testimony of Jesus (John 14:21, Revelation 1:9; 12:17; 14:12). Both are called saints (I Corinthians 6:1–2, Revelation 19:8; 13:7; 14:12; 17:6). Both are called God's servants (Romans 6:22, I Peter

2:16, Revelation 7:3; 19:2). Both are tied in with the Son of man (Acts 7:56, Revelation 1:13, 20b; Matthew 24:30; 25:31). Both are delivered from earthly troubles by Christ's coming in judgment (Acts 2:34–5, 3:20–1, II Thessalonians 1:7–10; 2:8, Matthew 25:31, Revelation 19:11–21). And both are included in the book of life (Philippians 4:3, Revelation 3:5; 13:8; 17:8).

The tribulation saints sure look like the church, don't they?

Pre-tribs declare that the word "church" isn't found in any earthly tribulation scenes in the book of Revelation. But they carefully avoid revealing that "church" is also not mentioned in any heavenly or in-the-air scenes in Revelation, chapters 4–19!

Commenting on the ninth chapter of the book of Daniel, Dwight Pentecost and other pre-trib writers say that since the church isn't described in the first sixty-nine weeks of Daniel's seventy weeks, it therefore will not be on earth during the seventieth week (great tribulation). Neither does Daniel 9:24–7 say anything about *Gentile* saints, which all agree will be here during the tribulation. Arguments from silence seldom carry much weight. But the point is this: the church *was* in existence when Jerusalem and its temple were destroyed (Daniel 9:26) and there is no good reason (and certainly no Bible verse) why God will have to cut off the church before Israel's reconciliation and righteousness (Daniel 9:24) are realized.

Pre-tribs also apply their argument of silence to Jeremiah 30:7 ("the time of Jacob's trouble"), which mentions neither the church nor Gentiles. They seemingly come to the conclusion that many more Gentile saints than church saints are born with the name of Jacob.

Apart from exegetical grounds, if pre-tribs *really* love Israel and Jewish persons, why don't they want to be around to encourage them during "the time of Jacob's trouble" and also rejoice with them when "everlasting righteousness" is accomplished?

I wouldn't want to miss it for anything—even a pre-trib rapture.

Was John Raptured?

Sensing that their dispensational program and Revelation 4–19 and some other passages fail to exempt the church from the days of Antichrist, pre-tribs then desperately try to prove a pre-trib rapture in Revelation 4:1. John was told "Come up hither. . . ." Did John really go up to heaven (as Hal Lindsey and some others affirm) and thus establish a "type" of the pre-trib rapture? If John *actually* went to heaven, it's strange that we find him back on earth in Revelation 10:1–2; 11:1–13; 13:1–18; 14:1, 19–20; 16; and 18:1. Was John raptured and then un-raptured a number of times?

If John was physically transported to heaven in 4:1, why was it necessary for him to be "in the Spirit" in 1:10? And if being "in the Spirit" in 1:10 doesn't imply a rapture, why should pre-tribs infer a rapture in 4:1–2 where John was in the same state of being?

Scofield notes (p. 1331) that John was merely "in the Spirit" in 4:1. Pentecost (*Things to Come*, p. 251) refers to John's catching up but doesn't explain it as either a physical or spiritual rapture. Walvoord, the president of the seminary Lindsey graduated from, writes in *The Revelation of Jesus Christ*, p. 103, that John was not raptured at this point and that his physical body remained on the island of Patmos.

The Restrainer

Although there is widespread disagreement as to who the "restrainer" is in II Thessalonians 2:7, many pre-tribs feel that he is the Holy Spirit. His partial removal from earth is accomplished, they argue, by the rapture of the believers whom He indwells. Thus they use even this passage in support of their doctrine.

But if the Holy Spirit's indwelling is missing during the tribulation, it would constitute a return to the "weak and beggarly elements" which Paul condemns as legalism (Galatians 4:9). The tribulation saints would then retreat from the Master to the schoolmaster. This would also mean that the 144,000, without the indwelling Holy Spirit, would better evangelize the world in seven years than the church has been able to do in nearly two thousand years *with* the indwelling Holy Spirit and *without* tribulation intensity all around.

If, on the other hand, pre-tribs concede that the tribulation saints are indwelt by the Holy Spirit, that damages their assertions about the Holy Spirit being the restrainer. If indwelt believers can't restrain the Antichrist later on, neither can the indwelt church now. All of which disproves the latter-day notion that the Antichrist can't appear while the church remains on earth.

Rapture versus Second Coming

Though all Bible passages dealing with the second coming consistently dovetail in real harmony with each other, some passages include certain details not found in other portions—details that are never canceled out by other verses.

Pre-tribs would have us believe that Christ meets us in the air, takes us to heaven for seven years, and then brings us back to earth after the tribulation. But I Thessalonians 4:17 doesn't say *where* we go after we meet the Lord in the air. And Zechariah 14:4 (when Christ stands on the mount of Olives) says nothing about the church being in heaven prior to that time.

This argument from silence is constantly used in a noisy way to try to prove that the rapture can't possibly happen at the second coming. Oliver B. Greene in his tract entitled *Rapture-Revelation-Kingdom* says that in I Thessalonians 4 there is "no battle, and no bloodshed." But the passage also omits the changing of bodies in the twinkling of an eye, the last trump, the dead being raised incorruptible, and the mortal putting on immortality. Pre-tribs know that these expressions are found in I Corinthians 15:51–3, which they say refers to the rapture. On the basis of different wording, does Greene believe that the coming in Thessalonians is not the same as the coming in Corinthians? Maybe he thinks there will be *two* pre-trib raptures.

Using the same reasoning, we could easily conclude that the gospels tell of more than one crucifixion and resurrection—perhaps more than one Jesus Christ—simply because some accounts give certain details not found in other accounts.

Only Matthew (27:3–10) tells of Judas returning the thirty pieces of silver and hanging himself.

Only in Luke (23:39–43) do we see the penitent thief promised paradise.

Only Matthew (27:62–6) tells of Pilate sending guards to Christ's tomb.

Only Mark (16:9–11) and John (20:11–18) record Christ's first post-resurrection appearance to Mary Magdalene.

Pre-tribs assert that the two stages (which should really be called *aspects*) are completely different, that Paul taught about the rapture while Christ taught about the second coming. And Walvoord (*The Rapture Question*, p. 148) insists that post-tribs have difficulty in harmonizing the rapture with the second coming.

Since Walvoord quotes Alexander Reese's *The Approaching Advent of Christ* many times he must be aware of the extensive chart Reese includes in his book on pp. 259–61, a chart showing that *every aspect* of the second coming Christ taught about can also be found in the epistles. (Reese lists fifty-three aspects along with Scripture references found in both the gospels and epistles.)

Christ and Paul both taught the same thing—a single future coming that is post-tribulational. Paul never contradicted anything taught by Christ; in I Thessalonians 4 Paul wrote: "For this we say unto you by *the word of the Lord. . . .*" A few verses earlier he had written: "For ye

know what commandments we gave you by *the Lord Jesus.*"
If a pre-trib rapture is the big thing we're looking and waiting
for, Christ gave no mention or hint of it in the gospels.

Types

Enoch, Noah, Lot, Joseph, and Elijah are sometimes seen
as types of the church being caught up before the tribulation
(although Margaret Macdonald included only Elijah in her
1830 pre-trib revelation account). But what about the
preservation of the three Jewish men in Nebuchadnezzar's
fiery furnace? And what about Daniel being preserved in the
den of lions? God didn't have to take them out of the world,
did He? My father *(Triumph Through Tribulation)* said it well,
"When will men cease carrying their little trays through the
cafeteria of Scripture, picking and choosing whatever strikes
their fancy?"

Day of the Lord

Pre-tribs know they can't separate the rapture from the
day of the Lord. So they stretch that day forward and hook it
up with their pre-trib rapture. But does the day of the Lord
include the tribulation, as they claim? Joel 2 says the cosmic
signs will happen *before* the day of the Lord, and even
Scofield ties in Matthew 24:29–30 with his Joel 2 notes. The
day of the Lord, therefore, starts at the *end* of the tribulation.

The Apostasy

In 1974, J. Vernon McGee stated on his *Through The Bible*
broadcast that the II Thessalonians 2:3 "falling away" is
really the rapture. E. Schuyler English futhered this idea in
his *Re-Thinking the Rapture*, pp. 67–71, in 1954. Roy L.
Aldrich, in the February 5, 1955 *Sunday School Times*,
referred to English's aberration as a *novel* view that hasn't
obtained general approval. And Walvoord *(The Rapture*

Question, p. 71) also speaks of English's *novel* explanation of this verse. English himself states in at least three places on p. 71 in his book that his interpretation is open to question and that he doesn't want to be dogmatic at this point.

But this argument is not novel, it is nonsensical. The passage clearly refers to the apostasy—a season of falling away from faith in God. The Greek word in question is *apostasia* and is variously translated "rebellion" (RSV), "Great Revolt" (JB), and "apostasy" (NASB).

Other Arguments

Pre-tribs often quote Revelation 3:10 in support of a pre-trib rapture. But much hinges on the meaning of the word "from" in the phrase "will keep thee from the hour of temptation." Henry Alford, the well-known Greek scholar, says "from (Greek *ek*) means *out of the midst of*: but whether by immunity from, or by being brought safe through, the preposition does not clearly define." The point is not indisputable, since the text speaks of the hour of trial that is coming on the whole world. However, *apo* would be a more suitable preposition. The use of *ek* in John 17:15b, Gal. 1:4 and Heb. 5:7 is illuminating in this regard.

Pre-tribs say that the "blessed hope" is a pre-trib rapture, or *first stage*. They add that the "glorious appearing" refers to the post-trib coming in judgment, or *second stage*, when Christ returns to earth *with* His saints. Both of these terms, however, are found in one verse, Titus 2:13, and both follow the expression "Looking for." This verse really says in the Greek (according to most Bible translations including Phillips, Wuest, Beck, Williams, RSV, NEB, Conybeare, Weymouth, Goodspeed, and Wade) that the blessed hope *is* the glorious appearing. (Pre-tribs also argue that a two-stage coming is taught in II Thessalonians 2:1-2.)

There are other pre-trib arguments, some of which will surface in other parts of this book.

One interesting sidelight of all this was aired not long ago over radio in Kansas City. A local pre-trib radio preacher who has a daily broadcast played "The King Is Coming" and then added: "Actually, folks, the theology in that song you just heard isn't too scriptural. When Christ comes as king, that's at the *end* of the tribulation. We're looking for the rapture *before* the tribulation."

With that in mind, maybe some pre-tribber will feel inspired to write a new song called "The Kidnapper Is Coming"!

13. THE MAJORITY VIEW

Some pre-tribs and post-tribs agree on at least one point. They think that the pre-trib rapture view is held by the *majority* of Bible-believing Christians. A few years ago I received a scorching letter from a pastor which said in part: "What amazes me is that you and your father . . . are the only ones that I know who hold such an unusual theory." He was, of course, referring to the post-trib view. In his letter he also listed thirteen well-known pre-trib leaders.

Later on, an associate of one of those thirteen leaders commented on that pastor's statement: "I would like to say that the man who wrote that letter certainly was not very well informed and certainly was out of step in calling it 'an unusual theory.'" Many Bible scholars, including some of pre-trib persuasion, have admitted in their writings that the post-trib rapture view is the *majority* view and always has been. As I have already mentioned, it was the *only* theory of the second coming before 1830. John F. Walvoord writes in *The Rapture Question*, p. 127, that the post-trib view is embraced by a majority in the church and has been around for a long time.

Herman A. Hoyt, president of Grace Theological Seminary in Winona Lake, Indiana, says practically the same thing in *The End Times*, p. 86. The executive editor of a popular pre-trib monthly magazine wrote in a letter: "We are, of course, well aware that many fine conservatives hold the post-tribulation rapture view." The editor of a widely distributed Southern Baptist publication said in a letter it is probable that there are more post-tribs among Southern Baptist pastors today than pre-tribs. And an article in the November, 1973, *Moody Monthly*, entitled "Curious About the Future?" by Moody Bible Institute professor Louis A. Barbieri, Jr., declared that pre-tribs are probably in the minority at the present time.

A top British scholar, a member of the Brethren, remarked in a letter: "In Brethren circles in Great Britain there are more younger men who do not hold the [pre-trib] view than older ones who will not give up the cherished notion passed by JND through Margaret Macdonald."

Post-mills and a-mills believe in a single coming of Christ when He will catch away the Church and punish the ungodly. But did you know that *most* scholars in the pre-mill division—where most of the controversy on this question takes place—are also post-trib?

Most Pre-Mills Are Post-Trib

In *The Second Coming Bible*, p. 385, William E. Biederwolf, the well-known evangelist who was also the president of the Winona Lake School of Theology, writes: "Godet, *like most pre-millennial expositors,* makes no provision for any period between the Lord's coming for His saints and His coming with them, and consequently refers the redemption of verse 28 [in Luke 21] and the elect of Matt. 24.31 to the saints in general, and not to the elect of Israel, as do Scofield, Pettingill, Gaebelein and others."

Incidentally, the editor-in-chief of a publishing firm that has reprinted some of Biederwolf's works told me that Biederwolf was definitely a post-trib. The list of several hundred eminent scholars in the back of *The Second Coming Bible* is almost solidly post-trib; in fact, I could find only about a dozen pre-tribs out of hundreds of names.

Post-trib leader Oswald J. Smith, in a pamphlet entitled *Tribulation or Rapture—Which?*, says he knows about seventy outstanding Bible teachers who are post-trib. On page 13 he writes:

> Among them . . . there are such names as W. J. Erdman, Charles R. Erdman, Dr. Campbell Morgan, Bishop Frank Houghton, Dr. A. B. Simpson, Dr. J. W. Thirtle, Dr. Charles T. Cook, Alexander Reese, Dr. Horatius Bonar, Dr. Adolph Saphir, Henry Varley, Dr. Nathaniel West, David Baron, H. W. Soltau, Dr. Bergin, Dr. Harold J. Ockenga, and many others.

Norman F. Douty's *Has Christ's Return Two Stages?* contains an extensive bibliography of the works of many post-trib authors including Alexander Fraser, Thomas Houghton, S. P. Tregelles, B. W. Newton, Frank H. White, H. L. Lindsay-Young, William J. Rowlands, Norman S. MacPherson (my father), Thomas Chalmers, and W. G. Moorehead, among others.

For about twenty-five years I've diligently tracked down outstanding post-tribs in all centuries from the time of Christ to the present day, and the total so far is well over a thousand. Here is a sampling: Henry Alford, Oswald T. Allis, Matthew Arnold, J. Sidlow Baxter, W. J. Ern Baxter, Del Birkey, F. F. Bruce, John Bunyan, Herbert W. Butt, John Calvin, Robert Cameron, Edward J. Carnell, Adam Clarke, Harry Conn, Alexander Cruden, Howard Ferrin, Charles Finney, George H. Fromow, John Gill, Jack Green, Robert H. Gundry, Roy E. Hayden, William Hendriksen, Carl F. H. Henry, Matthew Henry, Charles Hodge, Henry T. Hudson, Orson Jones, Russell B. Jones, Arthur D. Katterjohn, John Knox, C. S. Lovett, William G. Lowe, Martin Luther, J. Gresham Machen, S. I. McMillen, Robert E. McNeill, Robert C. McQuilkin, Dale Moody, Leon Morris, Iain H. Murray, Bernard Ramm, Harry Rimmer, R. J. Rushdoony, Ed F. Sanders, Charles Spurgeon, Edith Torrey (daughter of R. A. Torrey), B. B. Warfield, George Whitefield, Robert Dick Wilson, Robert Young, and Ronald F. Youngblood.

Silent Partners

Many Bible scholars of the present time have not wanted to be quoted even though they also see only a single future coming of Christ. For example, a popular preacher associated with a widely heard broadcast told me in a letter: "Most of my fellow workers and colleagues through the years have held to the pre-tribulation rapture and I have been able to work in real Christian fellowship with them even though I have not agreed with their prophetic positions."

The editor of an influential Christian magazine stated in a letter:

> I have reached the conclusion that the concept of a secret moment rapture as traditionally expressed by the dispensational viewpoint cannot be sustained in the light of current happenings. I believe that the Lucan prophecy that Jerusalem shall be trodden of the Gentiles until the times of the Gentiles has been fulfilled has itself now taken place with the re-establishment of the nation Israel and with the control of Jerusalem having passed into the hands of the Israelis. This I take to be actual fulfilled biblical prophecy. Since the traditional secret, any moment pretribulation rapture viewpoint holds that no known or predicted event can occur prior to the rapture of the church, then it is obvious that this is a known and predicted event which has actually transpired. Moreover, the destruction of Jerusalem was prophesied by our Lord Jesus Christ and actually took place in A.D. 70. This obviously means that between the time of the prediction and the time of the fulfillment there could have been no secret, any moment rapture of the church.

A top official connected with a worldwide broadcast, himself a post-trib, revealed in another letter that "I have often felt that this [post-trib] view is in the minority. Looking around and hearing many Christians expounding on prophecy, it appears on the surface that the majority are pre-tribulationists. Your long list of post-tribs certainly points to the fact that this is not true. . . . With the information having come from you the other morning, I will certainly feel more bold and forward in proclaiming what I have believed all these years."

I have corresponded with almost all forty-four contributing editors of *Christianity Today* and most of the men on that list have adopted the post-trib viewpoint. In fact, there are only two or three on the list who are still persistently pushing pre. A top Nazarene scholar told me that at a recent faculty meeting at the Nazarene Theological Seminary in Kansas City there was a consensus for the post-trib view. I have also discovered a good number of posts among the officials of the Full Gospel Business Men's Fellowship International.

Recently I was browsing in a Christian bookstore in Albuquerque, New Mexico. I chatted with the manager long enough to discover that she was an enthusiastic proponent of a pre-tribulational rapture—and she naturally assumed that her ideas were shared by the majority of the authors whose books she stocked in the store. Her eyes grew wide with amazement as we toured the aisles together and discovered that the vast majority of those volumes were authored by people who believed that the rapture and second coming were one and would happen after the great tribulation.

14. THE JEWS

Anti-Semitism is a very dirty word. The guilt and shame of its long history since the days of Queen Esther have been compounded in recent times by Russian pogroms and the Nazi holocaust. Men's hearts are as wicked as ever, but racism—including anti-Semitism—is out of fashion today.

Most pre-trib people, I am sure, would never knowingly oppose someone because he was Jewish. They are occasionally accused of it by Jews who resent their zealous evangelistic efforts, but, as Christians, we can understand this as a genuine expression of love towards Jews, not hate. Pre-trib literature abounds with a pro-Jewish sentiment that glorifies Israel. Reading it, one senses that the future belongs to that nation.

Hal Lindsey seems to carry this sentiment even a step further in his enthusiasm. In *There's a New World Coming* (p. 101) he asserts, like so many others, that the church must be removed from Earth before the emphasis can be shifted back to Israel. And yet, in *A Study Manual to The Late Great Planet Earth*, pp. 11 and 13, he says that Israel's political restoration in 1948 was "one of the most important events of our age" and "the most important prophetic sign to herald the era of Christ's return." In *The Late Great Planet Earth* he speaks of the "electrifying excitement" created by recent developments in Israel (p. 58). Lindsey has, I suggest, already shifted the emphasis back to Israel—almost as if the church were already translated to heaven.

But buried beneath much of the pre-tribulationists'

raptures over Israel is a subtle anti-Semitism. It is, explains Oswald T. Allis, "in a sense only the foil for the greater glorification of the Church" (*Prophecy and the Church*, p. 219). You can hear what Allis is talking about in these words by a preacher on a radio broadcast: "Now, beloved, the tribulation is the time of Jacob's trouble. That's for Israel and not for us. Praise God, we're going to be caught up *before* that awful time of judgment." If you're in the church listening to and believing things like this, it's difficult not to feel at least a little superior.

Yet many pre-trib advocates do seem to genuinely admire the modern Israelis. Indeed, their strength and courage in the face of Arab armies and terrorists is admirable. I think some of this Judophilism is motivated by the awareness of the church's flabby condition, especially in America. American middle-class life, which is, by and large, the life of American believers, is disappointingly materialistic and soft by biblical standards. It is not admirable; it doesn't produce heroes. Hence, the longing looks of men like Lindsey at the sturdy militance of Israel.

But the obvious answer lies in the serious renewal of the church, not enlistment in the Israeli army. We have already seen that the church is the Israel of God. That church already has and will continue to experience tribulation. Tribulation is one of God's agents for renewal; it inevitably has a cleansing effect on the church. Real men and women, solid disciples of Christ from Jewish and Gentile backgrounds will constitute the church in the great tribulation—a militant and vigorous church.

Jewish Ground?

I am part Jewish by birth and to me it's fantastic that many folks believe that the book of Matthew is on "Jewish" ground, that is, primarily dispensational and Jewish in content and outlook.

Pre-tribs maintain that the "elect" of Matthew 24 that go

through the tribulation is a Jewish remnant and not the church. Before 1830, however, Christians had always applied the term "elect" to themselves. Christians in A.D. 70, for instance, knew that they were the elect. As A. T. Pierson explains (*Many Infallible Proofs*, p. 67) "At this crisis, as we learn from church historians of the first century, all the followers of Christ took refuge in the mountains of Pella, beyond the Jordan, and there is no record of one single Christian perishing in the siege!"

The unbelieving Jews, on the other hand, did not heed the warnings of Matthew 24 or consider themselves the elect but stayed in Jerusalem and were slaughtered by the thousands.

If the Jewish Christians living in A.D. 70, many of whom had seen and talked with our Lord, knew that His church is the elect (for whom also the days of the tribulation are to be shortened), what right would anyone have in later years to disregard their understanding of Jesus' words?

The current teaching on the part of some that Matthew's gospel is "Jewish" (although inconsistently the "watch" verses and great commission *are* applied to the church) can be traced back to John N. Darby. But even he was unsure of himself on this point for quite some time. As the influential Brethren magazine *The Witness* editorialized in its July, 1972, issue, "Even Darby himself hesitated at the first before swallowing the view he afterwards held so tenaciously concerning the Gospel by Matthew as being Jewish and dispensational in character."

What the Chosen People Chose!

Most Christians are probably unfamiliar with the names of Neander, Rabinowitz, Schereschewsky, Caspari, and Biesenthal—all of them Jewish Christians of the nineteenth century. Others, like Baron, Delitzsch, Edersheim, and Saphir, are more familiar. Did you know that all of these great men were post-trib?

David Baron (1855–1926) wrote in *The Visions and Prophecies of Zechariah*, p. 323, that Paul "spoke of 'the blessed hope and the appearing of our great God and Saviour Jesus Christ' (Tit. ii.13), for then the hope as regards the church, and Israel, and the world, will be fully realised."

Compare Baron's statement with one by Walvoord in *The Rapture Question*, p. 81, which asserts that Israel and the world will not see the appearing of Christ when the church will.

Franz Delitzsch (1813–1890) was another eminent Hebrew Christian who failed to find a two-stage coming in Scripture. He also saw no distinction between the "day of Christ" and the "day of the Lord". In his *Commentary on the Epistle to the Hebrews*, Vol. II, p. 183, he said that "the approaching day is the day of Christ, who comes not now for atonement, but for final judgment."

Alfred Edersheim (1825–1889), whose writings are still widely read today, saw only one future coming of Christ which will be post-tribulational. In his massive work *The Life and Times of Jesus the Messiah*, Vol. II, pp. 451–2, he declared that "one might be taken up, the other left to the destruction of the coming Judgment. But this very mixture of the Church with the world in the ordinary avocations of life indicated a great danger . . . . We shall best succeed, not by going out of the world, but by being watchful in it."

Adolph Saphir (1831–1891) likewise saw the church enduring the last great struggle along with the believing Jewish remnant. In *The Epistle to the Hebrews*, Vol. I, p. 5, he wrote: "When the love of the majority shall wax cold, when iniquity shall abound, and the last struggle prepare, then let the church go on unto perfection, and behold with open face the glory of Christ; and, gazing on His brightness, she will be strong and courageous, and remain steadfast unto the end."

In the same work, pp. 95–6, Saphir added: "The 97th Psalm speaks of the advent of the Messiah, which is yet in the future, to which both the believing synagogue and the

Church of the Lord Jesus Christ are looking, when He is to be manifested in great power, and to be acknowledged as King of the whole earth."

Alexander Reese comments: "And if we may say that the new programme of the End [pre-trib dispensationalism] is repugnant to Hebrew tradition and ideals, it is noteworthy that, though the last hundred years have produced many eminent Hebrew Christians, not one of them has embraced the scheme under examination. The works of Adolph Saphir are deservedly held in high esteem by all well-read Darbyists; yet, though those writings reveal that Saphir was a close student of Darby, and was open to his better influence, he rejected his view of the End" (*The Approaching Advent of Christ*, p. 60).

A well-known leader in Jewish evangelism circles revealed in 1971 in a letter: "It was the impossibility of reconciling the [pre-trib] rapture teaching with the Scriptures that caused me to search the Scriptures, and I have moved more and more away from the dispensational approach which knows how to take the Bible apart but not how to put it together again! To me the second coming truth has lost none of its preciousness. On the contrary one can intelligently watch for Him to come."

To that I say Amen and Selah!

15. THE LINDSEY LEGEND

If any one person in our day has been successful in promoting the 145-year-old pre-trib rapture theory, it is Hal Lindsey. Let's do some backtracking to find out more about him.

Among *Christianity Today*'s choice evangelical books of 1972 was *The Jesus People: Old-Time Religion in the Age of Aquarius*, by Enroth, Ericson, and Peters. The magazine described it as "the most substantive" book about Jesus People. The ninth chapter of this book, entitled "The Last Days," points out that in recent years many Jesus People have become post-tribs. They haven't had a lot of money to buy theological works and Bibles with notes proclaiming a pre-trib rapture, but instead have had to rely upon inexpensive editions of the Word—and the Holy Spirit for its interpretation.

For years Dallas Theological Seminary had been aware of numbers of newly converted young people who had not been thoroughly indoctrinated in the pre-trib scheme of things. The situation was getting out of hand. What would happen to their militant pre-trib influence on many other Christian schools and numerous mission boards if a whole generation turned back to the historic post-trib view?

Was anyone around who was acquainted with the Jesus People movement and who could write up pre-trib in such a way that young people would go for it?

There was.

And he could.

What's more, the young man by the name of Hal Lindsey was a Dallas Seminary graduate.

Influenced by Pre-Tribs

There's no question that Lindsey has been greatly molded by pre-trib professors and writings. A careful check of the Dallas Seminary library card catalogue indicates an absence of post-trib subject matter. Not a single well-known post-trib book was listed, even though Walvoord, Pentecost, and their colleagues feel perfectly free to quote and mention such books in their writings.

The Dallas Seminary outlook is easily visible in Lindsey's books and he knows the value of plugging the literature of his former professors. (The school showed its appreciation by having him there as featured speaker during its recent 50th anniversary celebration.)

He also applauds C. I. Scofield whom he calls "the venerable old Bible scholar" (*There's A New World Coming*, p. 21). He has some nice words for the *New Scofield Reference Bible* on p. 39, and his application of the seven churches of Revelation to seven periods of church history closely parallels Scofield's, even to date-setting. Lindsey refers to Scofield's notes in *Satan Is Alive and Well on Planet Earth*, plugs Walvoord's *The Rapture Question* in his latest book, and acknowledges pre-trib works in all of his writings.

There is no doubt in my mind that his books have affected millions around the world. He is now quite famous, having been dubbed "the pied piper of the pre-trib rapture" and "the reincarnation of Scofield with longer hair." His books are packed with interesting quotes and generally worth-while information, but his devotion to a latter-day theory often leads him to make unscriptural comments and draw unfounded conclusions.

Flights of Fancy

Lindsey is completely taken up with the idea of a soon-to-happen, secret pre-trib rapture. So much so that his definition of the word "maranatha" on the last page of *The Late Great Planet Earth* comes out as "the Lord is coming soon." But language experts A. T. Robertson and Robert Young and many other scholars of note tell us that this expression means either "the Lord has come" or "the Lord will come."

On p. 143 in the same book, Lindsey shares his chief reason for holding to a pre-trib rapture. He says that if the rapture is at the same time as the second coming there will be no remaining mortals who are believers and therefore no one to enter the Kingdom and repopulate the earth. But he had already declared on p. 54 that a Jewish remnant, made up of mortals, *will* accept Christ at His post-trib revelation.

Pre-tribs, of course, constantly see Israel in the tribulation, even though there is no actual mention of it. But they say that the church isn't in the tribulation because the word "church" isn't specifically included in certain chapters of Revelation. *There's A New World Coming*, p. 78, tells us that the church "isn't mentioned *once* as being on earth from Chapters 4 through 19!" (The word "church", in the sense Lindsey is talking about, is also absent in Revelation 19:7–10 which tells about the marriage supper of the Lamb. Lindsey's argument, if applied to the marriage supper, could be called "The Case of the Missing Bride.")

On p. 142 in *The Late Great Planet Earth* he declares there is a great distinction between the church and Israel, that the church is fulfilling God's program today. He then says that the spotlight will once again shine upon the Jew during the tribulation—even though the word "Israel" is notably lacking from Revelation 7:4 to 21:12.

Lindsey says the "church" is mentioned nineteen times in Revelation 1–3, just before a so-called rapture in Revelation

4:1, but he doesn't tell us that when "church" is found in the first three chapters it is speaking about *local assemblies* and not about the universal body of believers. The lack of any mention of the worldwide body of Christ in the tribulation chapters in Revelation is really no big deal since it isn't specifically included in the first three chapters either.

Double Standard

Pre-tribs use any and all means to try to prove a pre-trib rapture. One of these is the double standard.

Lindsey gives us the impression that the tribulation is so horrible that the church could never go through it. What he really means is that the church wouldn't *want* to go through it. And, of course, if you don't want something badly enough you'll find ways to get out of it, right?

He naturally paints a terrible picture of the tribulation with phrases like: avalanche of judgment, ghastly pestilence, devastating judgments, mankind's darkest days, and incredible horrors. He calls it "a judgment so terrible that God isn't going to let His church go through it." But then he turns around in *The Late Great Planet Earth*, p. 143, and calmly says that during the tribulation "there will be people who will become believers" and moreover admits that "they will survive this terrible period of history," and on p. 111 adds that this period will see "the greatest number of converts in all history"—"so many . . . they can't be numbered."

What a double standard. The horrible time that the church couldn't possibly endure is overcome by "a great multitude, which no man could number" of Tribulation saints!

Twentieth century believers here in America would never have wanted to live in the first century and see Christ face to face because the package deal would also have included the first century persecutions. What a difference between present-day saints and first century saints who could be found "rejoicing that they were counted worthy to suffer shame for his name." Today many rejoice in the hope of escaping this world by means of a pre-trib rapture. Jesus prayed, ". . . not . . . that thou shouldst take them out of the world, but that thou shouldst keep them from the evil one."

More Discrepancies

In *There's A New World Coming*, pp. 77–8, Lindsey refers to the so-called *two stages* of Christ's return. He says that the two stages are different—one coming is "in the air" and the other is "to the earth." It is just as plausible to believe that He will return to the Earth via the air. Obviously Lindsey is arguing that He won't actually "touch down" in the first stage. But what proofs can he adduce to support this claim? Only, I fear, an argument from the silence of the Thessalonian passage. Lindsey's presuppositions about the whole matter keep him from conferring with other passages, for example Acts 1:11, which clearly indicate what the church has traditionally believed throughout most of its history— namely, that Christ will return to Earth by coming through the air.

Lindsey also insists that the first stage will be in "secret" while the second stage will be characterized by "every eye" seeing Him. The problem with this is that the New Testament does not use the word secret with reference to the coming of Christ (except, perhaps, with reference to its date). It does teach that He will return as a thief in the night which implies a degree of secrecy. But the texts (for example, Matthew 24:43 and I Thessalonians 5:2) explicitly use this phrase to indicate the unexpectedness of the day of the Lord and to warn believers to be alert and faithful in prayer.

Besides, something can be both secret and seen by all so long as deception is employed. Imagine a moving van stopping in front of your neighbor's house one sunny day. Two men get out, proceed in a leisurely fashion to take everything out of your neighbor's house, put it all in the van, and drive away. You don't give it a second thought. Later on, your neighbor comes home and starts yelling: "I've been robbed! They've taken everything!"

You saw the men, the van, and your neighbor's belongings, but at the time it didn't dawn on you who they were or what they were up to. That's the way it will be when Christ returns. Every eye will see Him, but many will not know who He is or what He is up to until it's too late. They won't escape.

When the sun is darkened, etc., we'll know that His coming is "even at the doors," but the world will be terrified and unable to explain such phenomena or realize their significance because it rejected the only Word outlining the future.

Of Thief I Sing

A Thief in the Night is a Christian film which portrays what some think will happen when Christ comes back for His church. It teaches a pre-trib rapture and says it will surprise Christians as "a thief in the night." However, *all* New Testament passages speaking of Christ coming as a thief are post-tribulational in context.

Matthew 24:43 (and the corresponding Luke 12:39) is tied in with the return of the king in glory (as Scofield puts it) which is necessarily post-tribulational within the pre-trib scheme itself (that is, this event is linked to the second stage by pre-trib teachers).

Both I Thessalonians 5:2 and II Peter 3:10 speak of the day of the Lord coming as a thief in the night. Scofield ties in these passages with the day of Jehovah, the day of the Lord, and the second coming of Christ in glory—again, a post-trib setting.

Revelation 3:3 says He will come as a thief to those who are defiled and not watching, and Revelation 16:15 is tied in with the great day of God Almighty and Armageddon—all clearly post-tribulational.

And I Thessalonians 5:2 is a verse that promises believers

that He will not come *secretly* upon them—which is just the opposite of the thrust of that new Christian film.

As someone has put it, "The *secret* pre-trib rapture is so secret that the church never heard of it for 1800 years."

16. A HOUSE DIVIDED

Ever since the pre-trib rapture theory ascended from the mists of western Scotland in the spring of 1830, there has been a good measure of disagreement about its meaning from within the ranks. One of the first disagreements took place in the new Brethren chapel in Plymouth, England, in 1831. There a Captain Percy Hall advanced the idea of a secret pre-trib rapture in a sermon he preached. This novel prophetic concept was ridiculed the same day by one of the members, George V. Wigram. (Harold Rowdon's *The Origins of the Brethren* has a complete discussion of the early days at Plymouth.)

At about the same time Robert Baxter, who joined Edward Irving's charismatic group in London in 1831, found himself soon disagreeing with Irving's newly-adopted view which saw some believers raptured up before the tribulation. He stated in his 1833 book *Narrative of Facts*, p. 17:

> An opinion had been advanced in some of Mr. Irving's writings, that before the second coming of Christ, and before the setting in upon the world of the *day of vengeance,* emphatically so called in the Scriptures, the saints would be caught up to heaven like Enoch and Elijah; and would be thus saved from the destruction of this world, as Noah was saved in the ark, and as Lot was saved from Sodom. This was an opinion I never could entertain; conceiving, as I did, that our refuge in and through the days of vengeance, would be some earthly sanctuary, until the Lord should come, the dead be raised, and those remaining alive should be caught up. (I Thess. iv. 17.)

Meanwhile back at the Brethren ranch the secret pre-trib rapture was facing increased opposition. Though J. N. Darby was toying with it, others were rejecting it. Some of the Brethren who either scorned it completely or later gave it up were Benjamin Newton, George Mueller, Henry Craik, James Wright, Robert Chapman, Henry W. Soltau, and Samuel P. Tregelles.

This pre-trib issue split the Brethren time and time again. In many Brethren groups in Great Britain a person was not considered "fundamentally sound" if he believed the church would be on earth during the days of Antichrist.

Alexander Reese, *The Approaching Advent of Christ*, p. 26, says this intolerant pre-trib attitude still exists in the twentieth century. He writes: "Anyone who denies the Church's immunity from the Antichristian persecution of the Last Days is looked upon as having departed seriously from the faith once delivered to the saints, and is received coldly or not at all by Darbyists. Thrice welcome is he who has written a tract affirming it."

Frank S. Mead's *Handbook of Denominations in the United States*, p. 58, remarks that the Brethren continued to splinter over this and other biblical issues when they spread to America in the late nineteenth century. He adds that there are eight bodies of Darbyist Brethren in the U.S. today, identified only by the Roman numerals I to VIII.

The Brethren influence on American evangelists and Bible teachers has been great. Scofield acknowledges this group in the front of his *Reference Bible* and has nice words for one of its members, Walter Scott.

Little Harmony

Not only did pre-tribs fail to see "eye to eye" at the very outset of their novel theory, but it's also true that pre-trib leaders in each generation since 1830 have had much occasion to differ among themselves on practically every crucial point in their prophetic scheme.

Pre-tribs like to say that no single verse proves a rapture before the tribulation. You have to put all the passages together, they say, to get the total picture. (But no amount of fancy juggling of 100 *black* pieces of a jigsaw puzzle can result in a *white* scene when put together.)

Right now let's follow their advice and critically take a look at the pieces in their dispensational puzzle and determine if there is any disharmony in their ranks.

Lindsey's Disagreements

Hal Lindsey, *There's A New World Coming*, p. 82, sees a secret pre-trib separation of believers and unbelievers in Matthew 24:40–41 ("one shall be taken, and the other left") and applies this passage to the church. But Dwight Pentecost, *Things to Come*, p. 162, says that one is taken for judgment while the other is left for a millennial blessing, and applies this post-trib passage to Israel and *not* to the church. Walvoord, *The Rapture Question*, pp. 109–10, sides with Pentecost against Lindsey.

Lindsey, *The Late Great Planet Earth*, p. 110, states that the "restrainer" of II Thessalonians 2:7 is the Holy Spirit. But Mrs. George C. Needham suggests that Satan could be the "restrainer" in her book, *The Antichrist*, p. 94. C. H. Mackintosh, *Papers on the Lord's Coming*, p. 49, believes it could be the Roman Empire. Hogg and Vine, in *The Epistles of Paul the Apostle to the Thessalonians*, pp. 259–60, see it as human law and order.

In *There's A New World Coming*, p. 75, Lindsey declares that John *actually left* the earth and went to heaven in Revelation 4:1. Scofield's notes, however, merely say that John was "in the Spirit" at that time. Walvoord, *The Revelation of Jesus Christ*, p. 103, also disagrees with Lindsey; Walvoord maintains that John was in his natural body on Patmos and was never actually raptured away.

Lindsey thinks that chapters 4–19 in Revelation make up the tribulation chapters (*There's A New World Coming*, p. 78).

But Scofield (*Reference Bible*, p. 1337) sees the tribulation in chapters 11–18, while William R. Newell says (*The Book of the Revelation*, p. 403) that the tribulation starts at chapter 13. Henry Thiessen's *Will the Church Pass Through the Tribulation?*, p. 20, declares the tribulation is found in chapters 6–19.

In *There's A New World Coming*, p. 85, Lindsey holds that the twenty-four elders in Revelation represent the church. Harry A. Ironside in his *Lectures on the Book of Revelation*, p. 82, views them as representative of both Old Testament and New Testament saints.

Lindsey (*There's A New World Coming*, p. 192) believes the second beast of Revelation 13 will be a Jew. Walvoord, however, states on p. 211 in *The Revelation of Jesus Christ* that there's no evidence that *either* of the Revelation 13 beasts is Jewish.

In *There's A New World Coming*, p. 66, he sees the tribulation in Revelation 3:10 and insists the church will be kept "out of it altogether." On pp. 70–71 in *The Rapture Question*, however, Walvoord writes that use of this text as proof of a pre-trib rapture may be debated.

Differences Galore

In *Things to Come*, p. 161, Pentecost says Luke 21:36 is not to be applied to the church. Walvoord, however, applies this verse to the church's *escape* on pp. 70, 142, and 194 in *The Rapture Question*, even though he also applies it inconsistently to the tribulation saints' *endurance* on p. 112.

Lewis Sperry Chafer sees a distinction between the "marriage supper" and the "marriage feast" in *Systematic Theology*, IV, p. 396. But Pentecost in *Things to Come*, p. 228, says the Greek doesn't distinguish between "marriage supper" and "marriage feast."

Scofield, *Reference Bible*, p. 915, declares that the verses in Matthew 24 that refer to the tribulation are 15–28. But Chafer's *Systematic Theology*, V, pp. 120–25, sees the tribulation in verses 9–26. E. Schuyler English states in *Re-Thinking the Rapture*, p. 43, that the tribulation verses here are verses 4–28. Theodore Epp, in *Rightly Dividing the Word*, p. 67, says verses 9–22. Arno C. Gaebelein, in *The Gospel According to Matthew*, II, p. 182, says verses 4–26.

Scofield maintains in his *Reference Bible*, p. 1212, that I Corinthians 1:8 ("day of our Lord Jesus Christ") is the same as the "day of Christ" or *first stage* of the second coming. C. H. Mackintosh disagrees (*Papers on the Lord's Coming*, p. 47) and affirms that this expression refers to the "day of the Lord" or *second stage*.

J. N. Darby's *Second Coming*, p. 84, ties in Isaiah 25:8 with I Corinthians 15:54 (as does Scofield in his *Reference Bible*, p. 734). On the same page Darby quotes Isaiah 25:5–8 and then adds: "That is at the time the resurrection takes place; for it is said in Corinthians, 'Then shall come to pass the saying which is written, Death is swallowed up in victory.' And thus it appears that the time when this resurrection takes place is the time when the Lord restores Israel, when He establishes Israel's place in Zion, and takes away the veil from off the face of all nations."

In other words, Darby said that the Old Testament saints will be resurrected when the church is raptured—which is true. Darby, of course, held to a pre-trib rapture, and since he knew that the resurrection is connected with the rapture, he naturally said that Israel will be raised from the dead *before* the tribulation. But Darby overlooked the fact that Israel is resurrected *after* the tribulation. Thus, at this point, he unwittingly put himself in the post-trib category.

Later pre-trib writers have seen this inconsistency in Darby's writings. Pentecost and others are aware that Israel will be raised after the tribulation, and further know that any tie-in of Israel's resurrection with the rapture is fatal to their theory. But, since Israel experiences its resurrection *after* the tribulation, pre-tribs feel they are forced to separate the rapture from the resurrection of the holy dead (*Things to Come*, p. 411)—something the church never dared to do for 1800 years!

My father, Norman S. MacPherson, recalls in his book *Triumph Through Tribulation* the 1942 New York Congress on Prophecy. One speaker referred to wars and social unrest of the day as significant signs for the church, while other speakers replied that signs are not for the church. Some said that the rapture is the same as the second coming, but another speaker told the audience that the rapture couldn't possibly be the second coming because Christ doesn't come all the way down to the earth at the rapture.

Recently David Webber proclaimed on his *Southwest Radio Church of the Air* broadcast that the Antichrist will be revealed to believers before they go up in the rapture. On the same day, however, broadcaster Oliver B. Greene stated on *The Gospel Hour* that the Antichrist will *never* be revealed to the church before the rapture.

Pentecost's *Things to Come* thoroughly documents pre-trib disagreements. In fact, it does such a good job that a student at a well-known pre-trib college told me it changed him over to post-trib.

Other books that cite many instances of pre-trib disharmony on crucial points of pre-trib doctrine include Oswald T. Allis' *Prophecy and the Church* (Presbyterian & Reformed), Loraine Boettner's *The Millennium* (Presbyterian & Reformed), Norman F. Douty's *Has Christ's Return Two Stages?* (Gibbs), Robert H. Gundry's *The Church and the Tribulation* (Zondervan), George E. Ladd's *The Blessed Hope* (Eerdmans), Norman S. MacPherson's *Triumph Through Tribulation* (author), J. Barton Payne's *The Imminent Appearing of Christ* (Eerdmans), and Alexander Reese's *The Approaching Advent of Christ* (Kregel).

17. THE GREAT COMMOTION

The pre-trib rapture view has been abandoned by so many persons in recent years that even Walvoord's *The Rapture Question*, which first came out in 1957, could not refrain from mentioning the present-day "resurgence" of the post-trib view on p. 127.

One well-known post-trib who used to be pre is Oswald J. Smith of Toronto. In his pamphlet *Tribulation or Rapture— Which?* Smith writes:

> Now, after years of study and prayer, I am absolutely convinced that there will be no rapture *before* the Tribulation, but that the Church will undoubtedly be called upon to face the Antichrist, and that Christ will come at the close and not at the beginning of that awful period. I believed the other theory simply because I was taught it by W. E. Blackstone in his book "Jesus Is Coming", the Scofield Reference Bible and Prophetic Conferences and Bible Schools; but when I began to search the Scriptures for myself I discovered that there is not a single verse in the Bible that upholds the pre-tribulation theory, but that the uniform teaching of the Word of God is of a post-tribulation rapture.

Years ago when I was a student at Wheaton College I asked president V. Raymond Edman for his viewpoint on the tribulation. He told me he was pre-trib. When I asked him why he believed it, this great man of God frankly admitted that he had been influenced by pre-trib books on hand and added that he hadn't found time to really check things out for himself.

Forgive Us Our Doubters

There are other pre-tribs, however, who've had serious doubts for years about their theory, but they continue to push it dogmatically anyway. A pastor here in the midwest said he's had doubts in his mind ever since his student days in Bible school, but you'd never know it by reading the paper he edits. Another pastor told me that he's almost a post-trib, but folks in his church get anything but that impression. What would happen to the pre-trib view overnight if all doubting pre-tribs suddenly made a clean break? We need more Oswald J. Smiths around—men who will admit they've been led down the primrose path of pre-tribulationism.

Allured Alumni

I have a long list of ex-Dallas Seminary men who are now post-trib. One of them is president of another seminary. And I get letters constantly from pastors all over who studied at pre-trib schools but later adopted the post-trib point of view.

Recently a Virginia pastor told me in a letter: "As a graduate of the Philadelphia College of Bible I had accepted the pre-trib rapture, but through the years of study of the Scriptures had come to the realization that there was no biblical basis for it."

Many who have studied at pre-trib schools are now reexamining their prophetic position. A top official in the Assemblies of God acknowledged in a letter: "Having been raised on the Scofieldian theory and being an alumnus of Dallas Seminary, my views on eschatology have been very strongly pre-tribulation. However, I am not hesitant to study the views of men who take a diverse view to mine."

Nathaniel West, in Reese's *The Approaching Advent of Christ*, p. 244, said, "The question is no longer a question of exegesis with such clear light before us. It is simply a question of ethics with every believer. Have we the right moral disposition toward the truth, or will we still cling to error because we have unfortunately defended it too long; shall we act against the Truth or for the Truth?"

On p. 284 of the same book Reese declares: "According to Darby and his followers, the Great Tribulation is the wrath of *God* against the Jewish people for their rejection of *Christ.* According to Scripture, it is the *Devil's* wrath against the saints for their rejection of *Antichrist,* and adherence to Christ. Let the reader once see the Scripture truth on this point, and the whole Darbyist case will be exposed as a campaign of assumptions, mis-statements, and sentiment."

A Dollar for Your Thoughts

Speaking of mis-statements, let's take a look at the book *A History of Fundamentalism in America* by George W. Dollar, chairman of the department of church history at Bob Jones University. As is the case with Hal Lindsey, the pre-trib rapture is a burning issue with Dollar. He draws attention to it and related points on at least forty-five pages. On pp. 72–3 Dollar has fairly reported the story of the old Niagara Bible Conference, "the greatest gathering of the saints of God on the continent" which met annually in the 1880s and 1890s. He acknowledges that pre-tribs and post-tribs worked together for many years until the issue of a pre-trib rapture divided and destroyed the conference; he points out that it was A. C. Gaebelein and his pre-trib group who wrecked Niagara and organized an "openly avowed pretribulational" conference at Sandy Cove.

Time and time again Dollar stresses a pre-trib rapture as if it's the most important doctrine in fundamentalism. On p. 231, in his section on Conservative Baptists, he evidently feels that premillennialism is weak if it doesn't include "the pretribulation rapture and the elements of dispensationalism." On p. 244, in a section on Freewill Baptists, he says one division is doctrinally fundamental—"even holding to the pretribulation rapture of the church. . . ."

In 1971 I received a letter from a former professor in the same school in which Dr. Dollar teaches. (I have omitted some names and dates in order to keep the letter writer anonymous.)

> I was brought up to be a strong pre-tribulationist. In fact I never even thought that the other view was worth inquiring into. When Dr. Bob Jones called me to teach in the Bob Jones College one of the first questions he asked me was whether I held to this view, and of course I said Yes. But while I was professor at the Bob Jones University, one of my colleagues ——— ——— happened to ask me if I had ever read anything on the post-trib side. I had to confess that I never had. He recommended two little books by ———. I read them and was truly astonished to find that the post-trib view is the simpler, more Scriptural, and more reasonable of the two. So I am now a post-tribulationist. Very interestingly, though, there was at that time on the BJU faculty a great scholar, Dr. Charles Brokenshire, who could teach 25 languages and every subject in the School of Religion. But he was a *post*-tribulationist. Dr. Jones considered him worth more than any other faculty member, perhaps worth more than all of us put together. During the school year 1954–55 Dr. Brokenshire died. After he died Dr. Jones went before his faculty meeting and announced that from that time on he would be true to his old-time promise to the Christians of America that he would strongly emphasize the *pre*-tribulation doctrine of the Second Coming of Christ and that he wanted all his teachers in the School of Religion to stand in favor of that doctrine! Thanks be to God, I am free to stand for my own convictions of what I believe to be true and right!

Go Read West, Young Man!

In his foreword to a reprint of Nathaniel West's *The Thousand Years*, pre-tribber Wilbur M. Smith describes West as a "scholar of unquestioned ability and deep insight into the Word of God." On p. 244 in *The Approaching Advent of Christ*, post-tribber Alexander Reese calls West "the most learned of American students of unfulfilled prophecy." On the same page Reese quotes West who once summed up the pre-trib rapture theory as

> the utterly unscriptural, any-moment theory of our Lord's second coming: a theory which makes of Christ and His apostles self-contradictory teachers, and of the scriptures wholly unreliable oracles. No delusion more pleasing and sweet on the one hand, or more wild, groundless, and injurious to truth and faith, on the other, has ever captivated the minds of men, than this one of an any-moment, unseen, secret advent, resurrection, and rapture, a delusion condemned and exposed on almost every page of the Word of God.

18. THE WAVE OF THE FUTURE

While pre-trib hold-outs are still as common as Scofield
Bibles, there is every indication that the post-trib view will
again assume a place of prominence in *all* Christian circles.
On recent trips across the U.S. I have found well-known
post-trib books in school libraries at Bob Jones University,
Tennessee Temple Schools, and John Brown University.

In October of 1971 a Dallas Seminary student told me in a
letter: "All of my contact with biblical instruction has been
from those who are of the pre-trib viewpoint. I have taken
the required eschatology course at DTS. During that course I
was exposed to the post-trib position. Some of my class-
mates, even now, are in or leaning toward that camp."

I am convinced that this student's experience is indicative
of the future. The pre-tribulational theory, in spite of the
enormous popularity of Hal Lindsey's books, is going to
continue to lose adherents. More and more Christians in
America and elsewhere are taking a sober look around
them—and a longer look at the New Testament. There are
signs all around us that God is pouring out His Spirit on all
flesh, that He is awakening His church out of her lethargy
and preoccupation with fanciful speculations. By His grace
He is helping us to take seriously the possibility that we will
be called upon to endure real suffering for His name—even
to pass through the great tribulation as His witnesses.

I pray that what I have shared in these pages will
encourage believers everywhere to take stock, and perhaps to
reconsider certain assumptions that have long been part of

the framework of their theology. But more, I pray that God's truth will prevail and that He will have His way in our lives—finding in us a readier obedience and trust than we have ever granted Him before.

Albury, dating back to the eleventh century, hosted early prophetic conferences in its huge library (below) from 1826 to
1830. (Both photos by A. H. Howick, Albury, Surrey.)

The shipbuilding town of Port Glasgow, Scotland, was the birthplace of the Pre-Trib Rapture theory in 1830. Port Glasgow's Newark Castle (below) guards a ship under construction while a freighter heads up the Clyde towards Glasgow.

Directly behind the author's wife, on the other side of Scotland's Gare Loch, stands the home of Isabella and Mary Campbell. J. N. Darby was a guest in the house (close-up below) in mid-1830.

Ireland's Powerscourt House, designed in 1730, saw other prophetic conferences in the 1830s. Robert Norton was curate at St. Matthew's (below) in Holbeck, England, from 1846 to 1854. (Above photo by the Irish Tourist Board.)

APPENDIX A
MARGARET MACDONALD'S ACCOUNT

[This is Margaret Macdonald's handwritten account of her 1830 Pre-Trib revelation, as included in Robert Norton's *Memoirs of James & George Macdonald, of Port-Glasgow* (1840), pp. 171–176. The italicized portions represent her account as it appears in shorter form in Norton's *The Restoration of Apostles and Prophets; In the Catholic Apostolic Church* (1861), pp. 15–18.]

"It was first the awful state of the land that was pressed upon me.[1] I saw the blindness and infatuation of the people to be very great. I felt the cry of Liberty just to be the hiss of the serpent, to drown them in perdition. It was just 'no God.' I repeated the words, Now there is distress of nations, with perplexity, the seas and the waves roaring, men's hearts failing them for fear—now look out for the sign of the Son of man. Here I was made to stop and cry out, O it is not known what the sign of the Son of man is; the people of God think they are waiting, but they know not what it is. *I felt this needed to be revealed, and that there was great darkness and error about it; but suddenly what it was burst upon me with a glorious light. I saw it was just the Lord himself descending from Heaven with a shout, just the glorified man, even Jesus; but that all must, as Stephen was, be filled with the Holy Ghost, that they might look up, and see the brightness of the Father's glory. I saw the error to be, that men think that it will be something seen by the natural eye; but 'tis spiritual discernment that is needed, the eye of God in his people. Many passages were revealed, in a light in which I had not before seen them. I repeated, 'Now is the kingdom of Heaven like unto ten virgins, who went forth to meet the Bridegroom, five wise and five foolish; they that were foolish took* their lamps, but took no oil with them; but they that were wise took oil in their vessels with their lamps.' 'But *be ye not unwise, but understanding what the will of the Lord is; and be not drunk with wine* wherein is excess, *but be filled with the Spirit.'* This was *the oil the wise* virgins *took in their vessels—this is the light to be kept burning—the light of God—that we may discern that which cometh not with observation to the natural eye. Only those who have the light of God within them will see the sign of his appearance. No need to follow them who say, see here, or see there, for his day shall be as the lightning to those in whom the living Christ is.* 'Tis Christ in us that will lift us up—he is the light—'tis only those that are alive in him that will be caught up to meet him in the air. *I saw that we must be in the Spirit, that we might see spiritual things. John was in the Spirit, when he saw a throne set in Heaven.—But I saw that the glory of the ministration of the Spirit had not been known. I repeated frequently,* but *the spiritual temple must and shall be reared, and the fulness of Christ* be *poured into his body, and then shall we be caught up to meet him.* Oh *none will be counted worthy of this calling but his body,* which is *the church,* and which must be *a candlestick all of gold.* I often said, *Oh the glorious inbreaking of God* which is *now about to burst on this earth;* Oh *the glorious temple* which is *now about to be reared, the bride adorned for her husband; and Oh what a holy, holy bride she must be, to be prepared for such a glorious bridegroom.* I said, Now shall the people of God have to do with realities—*now shall the glorious mystery of God in our nature be known—now shall it be known what it is for man to be glorified.* I felt that the revelation of Jesus Christ had yet to be opened up—it is not knowledge about God that it contains, but it is an entering into God—I saw that there was a glorious breaking in of God to be. *I felt as Elijah, surrounded with chariots of fire. I saw as it were, the spiritual temple reared, and the Head Stone brought forth with shoutings of grace, grace, unto it. It was a glorious light above the brightness of the sun, that shone round about me. I felt that those who were filled with the Spirit could see spiritual things, and feel walking in the midst of them, while those who had not the Spirit could see nothing—so that two shall be in one bed, the one taken and the other left,* because the one has the light of God within while the other cannot see the Kingdom of Heaven. *I saw the people of God in an awfully dangerous situation,* surrounded by nets and entanglements, about to be tried, and many about to be deceived and fall. *Now will THE WICKED be revealed, with all power and signs and lying wonders, so that if it were possible the very elect will be deceived.*—This is the fiery trial which is to try us.—It will be for the purging and purifying of the real members of the body of Jesus; but Oh *it will be a fiery trial. Every soul will be shaken to the very centre.* The enemy will try to shake in every thing we have believed—*but the trial of real faith will be found to honour and praise and glory. Nothing but what is of God will stand. The stony-ground hearers will be made manifest—the love of many will wax cold. I* frequently *said* that night, and often since, *now shall the awful sight of a false Christ be seen on this earth, and nothing but* the living *Christ in us can detect this awful attempt of the enemy to deceive—for it is with all deceivableness of unrighteousness he will work—he will have a counterpart for every part of God's truth, and an imitation for every work of the Spirit.* The Spirit must and will be poured out on the church, that she may be purified and filled with God—and just *in proportion as the Spirit of God works, so will he—when our Lord anoints men with power, so will he. This is* particularly the nature of *the trial, through which those are to pass who will be counted worthy to stand before the Son of man. There will be outward trial* too, *but* 'tis *principally temptation. It is brought on by the outpouring of the Spirit, and will* just *increase in proportion as the Spirit is poured out.* The trial of the Church is from Antichrist. It is by being filled with the Spirit that we shall be kept. *I frequently said, Oh be filled with the Spirit—have the light of God in you, that you may detect satan—be full of eyes within—be clay in the hands of the potter—submit to be filled,* filled *with God.* This will build the temple. *It is not by might nor by power, but by my Spirit, saith the Lord. This will fit us to enter into the marriage supper of the Lamb. I saw it to be the will of God that all should be filled. But what hindered the* real *life of God from being received by his people, was their turning from Jesus,* who is the way to the Father. They were not entering in by the door. For he is faithful who hath said, by me if any man enter in he shall find pasture. They were *passing the cross, through which every drop of the Spirit of God flows to us.* All power that comes not through the blood of Christ is not of God. When I say, they are looking from the cross, I feel that there is much in it—they turn from the blood of the Lamb, by which we overcome, and in which our robes are washed and made white. There are low views of God's holiness, and a ceasing to condemn sin in the flesh, and a looking from him who humbled himself, and made himself of no reputation. *Oh! it is* needed, *much needed* at present, *a leading back to the cross. I saw that night, and often since, that there will be an outpouring of the Spirit* on the body, *such as has not been, a baptism of fire, that all the dross may be put away.* Oh there must and will be such an indwelling of the living God as has not been—*the servants of God sealed in their foreheads*—great conformity to Jesus—*his holy* holy *image* seen *in his people*—just *the bride made comely, by his comeliness put upon her.* This is what we are at present made to pray much for, that speedily we may all be made ready to meet our Lord in the air—and it will be. *Jesus wants his bride. His desire is toward us. He that shall come, will come, and will not tarry.* Amen and Amen. Even so come Lord Jesus."

Several observations are in order:

First of all, she evidently did not believe in imminence; she thought that "the fulness of Christ" (Spirit-filling) was first necessary— "and then shall we be caught up to meet him." She said that the catching up (or Rapture) would be seen only by Spirit-filled believers—a secret coming.

She equated the "sign of the Son of man" (which is in a Post-Trib setting in Matt. 24:30) with "the Lord himself descending from Heaven with a shout" (I Thess. 4:16). Either her Tribulation occurs in a short space at the very end of the age (highly unlikely considering the fiery trial that would purge those in the church "who had not the Spirit"), or else she thought that the sign of the Son of man, though unseen by the world, will be seen by Spirit-filled believers before "THE WICKED be revealed"; she apparently believed the latter interpretation.

When she spoke of "one taken and the other left" it was not a separation of believers and unbelievers but rather Spirit-filled believers taken while believers not filled with the Spirit are left. But the point is this: some are to be taken (in a Rapture) *before* "THE WICKED" (or Antichrist) is revealed; when she used the term "Now" in her expression "Now will THE WICKED be revealed," she meant "later" or "after this" and was using this term sequentially. (J. N. Darby used the same word in the same way in his quote in the fifth chapter of this book: "Now He was Himself manifested. . . .")

Margaret believed that a select group of believers would be raptured from the earth before the days of Antichrist, but also saw other believers enduring the Tribulation; she divided up the last generation of believers while Darby at least kept the church intact—but exempted all of the church from the Tribulation. In footnote 5 in chapter 5, Robert Norton elaborated on the doctrine that sprang from Margaret's revelation, and in chapter 6 he declared that Margaret's statement was the *first* instance of two-stage teaching.

The above evidence in published form has been shared in recent months with evangelical scholars around the world. In his book *The Church and the Tribulation*, Westmont College professor Robert H. Gundry originally leaned towards Edward Irving as the pre-trib originator. (His latest printing, however, deleted all of his Irving support and substituted the facts about Margaret Macdonald as found in this book.)

Later on J. Barton Payne described our evidence, in an *Evangelical Theological Society Journal* review, as "the most in-depth study yet to be made available on the historical origins of pretribulationism." *The Witness*, oldest and largest Darbyist Brethren magazine in England, admitted in a review last year that the above evidence "succeeds in establishing that the view outlined was first stated by a certain Margaret Macdonald"—despite those who still say that the Apostle Paul was first. And F. F. Bruce recently summed up our discoveries in *The Evangelical Quarterly* as a "valuable and racy narrative, which students of nineteenth-century prophetic interpretation are bound to take seriously."

Since Margaret Macdonald was the first person to teach a

coming of Christ that would precede the days of Antichrist, it necessarily follows that Darby—back to whom pre-tribism can easily be traced—was at least second or third or even farther on down the line. To date no solid evidence has been found that proves that anyone other than this young Scottish lassie was the first person to teach a future coming of Christ before the days of Antichrist. Before 1830 Christians had always believed in a single future coming, that the catching up of I Thess. 4 will take place after the Great Tribulation of Matthew 24 at the glorious coming of the Son of man when He shall send His angels to gather together all of His elect.

Whether she realized it or not, Margaret did her part to pave the way for doctrine that would demand separate waiting rooms at the end of this age—one for the church and another one for Israel!

Finally, to charge that Darby could never have been influenced by Margaret's pre-Antichrist rapture, with the knowledge of her revelation and his whereabouts in 1830 now out in the open, is practically the same as saying that a man found with a smoking revolver in hand and standing over a freshly killed victim in the middle of a lonely desert could not possibly be a suspect!

NOTES

1. At the end of this first sentence Norton adds a footnote which is explained at the bottom of p. 171: "I think I ought not to omit stating that in the course of the memorable evening of which the above paper is a very incomplete outline, one individual was expressly mentioned by name as the future desolator of this land, who at the time (nine years ago) was not at all pre-eminent as the leader of infidelity, but who has since so notoriously and awfully become so—Mr. Owen." The Owen referred to was Robert Owen (1771–1858), described by Friedrich Engels in his *Socialism: Utopian and Scientific* (1880) as one of the leading socialists of the early nineteenth century. A lengthy article on the editorial page of the January 10, 1973, *Kansas City Star* entitled "Tracing the History of Communes" says Owen established a number

of communities that were Communistic in nature. He set up communes in Ireland and Britain; his best-known commune, however, was his American community at New Harmony, Indiana. Margaret, on the same evening she had her pre-trib revelation, mentioned Owen as the future desolator, or Antichrist.

APPENDIX B
BIBLIOGRAPHY OF WORKS CITED
AND CONSULTED

Allis, Oswald T., *Prophecy and the Church*. Nutley, New Jersey: The Presbyterian and Reformed Publishing Co., 1945.

Anderson, John A., *Heralds of the Dawn*. Aberdeen, Scotland: Author, 1946.

Bass, Clarence B., *Backgrounds to Dispensationalism*. Grand Rapids: Wm. B. Eerdmans Publishing Co., 1960.

Baxter, Robert, *Narrative of Facts, Characterizing the Supernatural Manifestations in Members of Mr. Irving's Congregation, and Other Individuals, in England and Scotland, and Formerly in the Writer Himself*. London: James Nisbet, 1833.

Berkhof, L., *The Second Coming of Christ*. Grand Rapids: Wm. B Eerdmans Publishing Co., 1960.

Blackstone, W. E., *Jesus Is Coming*. New York: Fleming H. Revell Co., 1932.

Boase, C. W., *Supplementary Narrative to the Elijah Ministry*. Printed privately and posthumously, 1868.

Boase, Frederic, *Modern English Biography*. London: Frank Cass & Co., 1965.

Boettner, Loraine, *The Millennium*. Nutley, New Jersey: The Presbyterian and Reformed Publishing Co., 1957.

Christenson, Larry, *A Message to the Charismatic Movement*. Minneapolis: Bethany Fellowship, 1972.

Coad, F. Roy, *A History of the Brethren Movement*. Grand Rapids: Wm. B. Eerdmans Publishing Co., 1968.

Craig, Edward, *A Letter to Thomas Erskine, Esq., in Reply to his Recent Pamphlet in Vindication of the West Country Miracles*. Edinburgh: William Oliphant, 1830.

Darby, J. N., *Collected Writings of J. N. Darby*, edited by William Kelly, n.d. Oak Park, Illinois: Bible Truth Publishers, reprint 1972.

——, *Letters of J. N. D.* Oak Park, Illinois: Bible Truth Publishers, reprint 1971.

Douty, Norman F., *The Great Tribulation Debate: or, Has Christ's Return Two Stages?* Harrison, Ark.: Gibbs Publishing Co., 1975.

Drummond, A. L., *Edward Irving and His Circle.* London: James Clarke & Co., n.d. [circa 1937].

Ebaugh, David P., *Who Said Rapture?* Harrisburg, Pennsylvania: Author, n.d.

Edwards, Wesley G., *The Day of Vengeance.* Los Angeles: Author, n.d. [circa 1964].

English, E. Schuyler, *Re-Thinking the Rapture.* Neptune, New Jersey: Loizeaux Brothers, 1954.

Enroth, Ronald M./Edward E. Ericson, Jr./C. Breckinridge Peters, *The Jesus People.* Grand Rapids: Wm. B. Eerdmans Publishing Co., 1972.

Erskine, Thomas, *On the Gifts of the Spirit.* Greenock, Scotland: Author, 1830.

Fromow, George H., *Will the Church pass through the Tribulation?* Author, n.d.

Froom, LeRoy E., *The Prophetic Faith of Our Fathers.* Washington, D. C.: Review & Herald Publishing Association, 1950.

Fuller, Daniel P., *The Hermeneutics of Dispensationalism.* Pasadena, California: Fuller Seminary, 1966.

Graham, Billy, *World Aflame.* Garden City, New York: Doubleday & Co., 1965.

Graham, James R., *Watchman, What of the Night?* Minneapolis: Men For Missions reprint, n.d.

Greene, Oliver B., *Rapture-Revelation-Kingdom.* Greenville, South Carolina: Author, n.d.

Gundry, Robert H., *The Church and the Tribulation.* Grand Rapids: Zondervan Publishing House, 1973.

Hamilton, Floyd, *The Basis of Millennial Faith.* Grand Rapids: Wm. B. Eerdmans Publishing Co., 1942.

Henry, Carl F. H., *The Barbarians Are Coming. Eternity* magazine reprint, 1970.

Humbard, Rex, *The Absolute Certainty of Jesus' Coming Again.* Akron, Ohio: Author, 1971.

Ironside, H. A., *Not Wrath, But Rapture.* Neptune, New Jersey: Loizeaux Brothers, n.d.

Katterjohn, Arthur, *The Rapture—When?* Wheaton, Illinois (220 E. Union, 60187): Author, n.d.

———, *The Tribulation People.* Carol Stream, Illinois: Creation House, 1975.

Kelly, W., *The Rapture of the Saints: Who Suggested It, or Rather on What Scripture?* London: T. Weston, 1903.

Kraus, C. Norman, *Dispensationalism in America.* Richmond: John Knox Press, 1958.

Kromminga, D. H., *The Millennium in the Church.* Grand Rapids: Wm. B. Eerdmans Publishing Co., 1945.

Lacunza, Manuel de (pen name, Juan Josafat Ben-Ezra), *The Coming of Messiah in Glory and Majesty translated from the Spanish with a preliminary discourse by the Rev. Edward Irving, A.M.* London, 1827.

Ladd, George E., *Crucial Questions About the Kingdom of God.* Grand Rapids: Wm. B. Eerdmans Publishing Co., 1952.

———, *The Blessed Hope.* Grand Rapids: Wm. B. Eerdmans Publishing Co., 1956.

LaHaye, Tim, *The Beginning of the End.* Wheaton, Illinois: Tyndale House Publishers, 1972.

Lang, G. H., *The Revelation of Jesus Christ.* London: Oliphants, 1945.

Lindsey, Hal/C. C. Carlson, *The Late Great Planet Earth.* Grand Rapids: Zondervan Publishing House, 1970.

Logsdon, S. Franklin, *Profiles of Prophecy.* Grand Rapids: Zondervan Publishing House, 1970.

Ludwigson, R., *A Survey of Bible Prophecy.* Grand Rapids: Zondervan Publishing House, 1973.

MacArthur, William F., *History of Port Glasgow.* Glasgow: Jackson, Wylie & Co., 1932.

MacPherson, Norman S., *Tell It Like It Will Be.* Albuquerque, New Mexico: (516 Doe Lane S.E., 87123): 1970.

———, *Triumph Through Tribulation.* Otego, New York: Author, 1944.

McDougall, Duncan, *The Rapture of the Saints.* Blackwood, New Jersey: Old Fashioned Prophecy Magazine Publishers, reprint 1970.

McMillen, S. I., *Discern These Times.* Old Tappan, New Jersey: Fleming H. Revell Co., 1971.

Miller, Edward, *The History and Doctrines of Irvingism.* London: C. Kegan Paul & Co., 1878.

Murray, Iain H., *The Puritan Hope.* London: The Banner of Truth Trust, 1971.

Neatby, William B., *A History of the Plymouth Brethren.* London: Hodder and Stoughton, Publishers, 1901.

Newman, F. W., *Phases of Faith.* London, 1850.

Norton, Robert (R. N.), *A Discourse on the Faith and Hope of the Catholic Apostolic Church.* London: Thomas Bosworth, 1854.

———, *Agnus Dei: The Lamb of God.* London: Thomas Bosworth, 1867.

———, *Memoirs of James & George Macdonald, of Port-Glasgow.* London: John F. Shaw, 1840.

———, *Neglected and Controverted Scripture Truths; With an Historical Review of Miraculous Manifestations in the Church of Christ; and an Account of Their Late Revival in the West of Scotland.* London: John F. Shaw, 1839.

———, *Primary Truths of Christianity: for "The Hour of Temptation".* London: Thomas Bosworth, 1878.

Norton, Robert (R. N.), *Reasons for Believing that The Lord has Restored to the Church Apostles and Prophets.* Author, 1852.

————, *The Antitype of the Passover in the Worship of Christian Families.* London: Thomas Bosworth, 1852.

————, *The Restoration of Apostles and Prophets; In the Catholic Apostolic Church* (pamphlet). London: T. Bosworth, 1854.

————, *The Restoration of Apostles and Prophets; In the Catholic Apostolic Church* (book). London: Bosworth & Harrison, 1861.

————, *The Nearness of the Second Coming of Christ.* London: Thomas Bosworth, 1852.

————, *The True Position and Hope of the Catholic Apostolic Church.* London: Thomas Bosworth, 1866.

————, *Truths and Untruths; Respecting a Restored Apostolate.* London: Thomas Bosworth, 1876.

Oliphant, Margaret O. W., *The Life of Edward Irving.* London: Hurst and Blackett, Publishers, 1865.

Payne, J. Barton, *Encyclopedia of Biblical Prophecy.* New York: Harper & Row, 1973.

————, *The Imminent Appearing of Christ.* Grand Rapids: Wm. B. Eerdmans Publishing Co., 1962.

Pentecost, J. Dwight, *Things to Come.* Findlay, Ohio: Dunham Publishing Co. (Zondervan Publishing House), 1958.

Reese, Alexander, *The Approaching Advent of Christ.* Grand Rapids: Grand Rapids Intern. Publications (Kregel), 1975.

Roberts, Alexander/James Donaldson, *The Ante-Nicene Fathers.* New York: Charles Scribner's Sons, 1886.

Rowdon, Harold H., *The Origins of the Brethren.* London: Pickering & Inglis, 1967.

Rowlands, William J., *Our Lord Cometh.* London: The Sovereign Grace Advent Testimony, 1964.

Ryrie, Charles C., *The Basis of the Premillennial Faith.* Neptune, New Jersey: Loizeaux Brothers, 1953.

Sandeen, Ernest R., *The Roots of Fundamentalism.* Chicago: The University of Chicago Press, 1970.

Schaeffer, Francis A., *The Church at the End of the 20th Century.* Downers Grove, Illinois: Inter-Varsity Press, 1970.

Scofield, C. I., *The Scofield Reference Bible.* New York: Oxford University Press, 1917.

Scruby, Moreton F., *Immediately After the Tribulation.* Dayton, Ohio: John J. Scruby Printing Co., 1951.

Shaw, P. E., *The Catholic Apostolic Church.* Morningside Heights, New York: King's Crown Press, 1946.

Smith, Oswald J., *Prophecy—What Lies Ahead?* London: Marshall, Morgan & Scott, 1969.

————, *Tribulation or Rapture—Which?* London: The Sovereign Grace Advent Testimony, n.d.

Stanton, Gerald B., *Kept From The Hour.* Grand Rapids: Zondervan Publishing House, 1956.

Story, Robert, *Peace in Believing, or Memoirs of Isabella Campbell,* 1829.

Strachan, Gordon, *The Pentecostal Theology of Edward Irving.* London: Darton, Longman, & Todd, 1973.

Tregelles, S. P., *The Hope of Christ's Second Coming.* London: Samuel Bagster and Sons, 1864.

Walvoord, John F., *The Rapture Question.* Findlay, Ohio: Dunham Publishing Co. (Zondervan Publishing House), 1957.

Warfield, B. B., *Miracles: Yesterday and Today.* Grand Rapids: Wm. B. Eerdmans Publishing Co., reprint 1953.

White, John Wesley, *Re-entry!* Grand Rapids: Zondervan Publishing House, 1970.

Whitley, H. C., *Blinded Eagle.* London: SCM Press, 1955.

Woodhouse, Francis V., *A Narrative of Events Affecting the Position and Prospects of the Whole Christian Church.* Printed privately, 1885.

APPENDIX C

RECOMMENDED BOOKS
BY DR. JAMES McKEEVER

I have recently come into contact with James McKeever, an author whom I respect a great deal and in whose writings and ministry I have much confidence.

James has searched the Scriptures diligently and has come up with a solid biblical basis for believing that Christians will indeed go through the tribulation. He also has very practical wisdom to impart on things one can do physically and spiritually to prepare for the tribulation. I consider his book, *CHRISTIANS WILL GO THROUGH THE TRIBULATION—And how to prepare for it*, a must reading for every Christian. When I first ran across this book, I sent him a letter telling him that the body of Christ needed more from his pen.

James has come out with another book entitled *Revelation for Laymen.* This book gives much insight into the book of Revelation and clears up many of the things that have been confusing to people in times past. I think he has done a marvelous job in this work. As the tribulation draws nearer, understanding the book of Revelation could be a matter of survival for Christians. I recommend this book highly, and encourage you to understand the book of Revelation.

I labored almost alone for years, trying to alert the body of Christ to the fact that Christians will indeed go through the tribulation. It is encouraging to me to see outstanding Christian leaders such as Pat Robertson, Corrie Ten Boom, Jim Spillman, and others join our ranks in warning the body of Christ. I am especially pleased to have a man of the stature, the international reputation and the high calibre of James McKeever to add his voice to this growing chorus of those warning the body of Christ to prepare for the tribulation. I highly recommend his writings and cassettes to you.

There is one of James McKeever's writings that I would especially recommend, and that is his newsletter, *End-Times News Digest (END)*. This monthly newsletter gives an up-to-the-minute commentary on current events as they relate to the end times and Bible prophecy. I have found it a source of help, understanding, and inspiration in my own life. A Christian today should certainly be receiving this publication, which I am confident will be a tremendous help as the tribulation gets nearer.

On the following pages are descriptions of some of James McKeever's books and the *End-Times News Digest*. I hope that you will prayerfully consider them, for I believe they can be a real blessing and help to you.

PREPARING FOR EMERGENCIES

By Dr. James McKeever
With Jeani McKeever

We are sure you would agree that every family needs to be prepared for disasters and emergenices, but you may not know where to begin. *Preparing For Emergencies,* the first in this series on "Preparation," tells you exactly where to begin in terms of preparation and where to go from there.

Major disasters, such as earthquakes, tornadoes, hurricanes, winter storms, fires, floods, riots, robberies, terrorist bombings, fires and nuclear explosions *can strike suddenly.* In fact, one of these disasters could strike any place on planet earth at any time. Your home is no exception.

This practical book helps you anticipate emergency conditions, equips you to better handle disasters, gives advice on numerous related topics, such as storage of water and food, as well as how to maintain a source of light, heat and shelter. Written in priority sequence, it gives you an easy plan to follow, to whatever level of preparedness you feel prompted to go. It is an invaluable compilation of years of research and down-home experience, including an Appendix worth the price of the book! It lists sources where you can buy numerous items you would need to prepare for emergency situations. This important book is a *must!*

— — — — — — — — — — — — — — — — —

Omega Publications   BC-126
P.O. Box 4130
Medford, OR 97501

Please send me _____ copies of *Preparing For Emergencies* ($11.99 each). Enclosed is $_____.

Name_____

Address_____

City, State_____ Zip _____

MORE ON THE RAPTURE

Hosts of Christians around the world believe that we are living in the end times. There has been a need for a book that clearly outlines what the Bible has to say about the rapture, the return of our Lord and Savior Jesus Christ and end-times events in general. *Here is that book.*

Most Christians are very unknowedgeable as to how the Bible says this age will end. Because of this lack of knowledge, many Christians will go through the end of this age in defeat and despair. However, God has made a provision so that we can go through what lies ahead with real power and victory. We *can* experience triumph rather than defeat. We *can* experience jubilation rather than despair.

This book tells you how you can become part of the victorious end-time army of Jesus Christ and go through the end of this age as an overcomer.

Evangelist Jim Spillman says, "It is rare indeed for our searching eyes and hungry hearts to come upon a book that is at once forthright, persuasive and fully clothed with the word of God . . . The subject of this book has more of a need to be taught today to Christians than any other that I can think."

REVELATION FOR LAYMEN

By Dr. James McKeever

At last! . . . A clear, readable study of the Book of Revelation, geared for plain folks.

In both the first and last chapters of Revelation there is a blessing promised to those who read and *heed* the words contained in Revelation. This book concentrates on the "heed" aspect. How do you *heed*—incorporate into your daily life—the things found in the book of Revelation? God commanded us to do this, so there must be some things in there that we need to practice daily.

In times past, understanding and heeding the book of Revelation was almost optional for a Christian. But, in the light of recent world events, understanding the book of Revelation has become critical and essential to our understanding of what is happening in the world today, where we are going, and what we should do.

Satan does not want you to read the book of Revelation. He wants you to be confused by the conflicting interpretations of it. But God wants you to read it, to understand it, *and to act on what it says.* McKeever helps to make Revelation an exciting and understandable book, and an essential guide to survival in these end times.

— — — — — — — — — — — — —

Omega Publications   B4-101
P.O. Box 4130, Medford, Oregon 97501

I am enclosing the amount shown below for _____ copies of
REVELATION FOR LAYMEN:

_____ Copies of hardback at $14.99 each = $ _____

_____ Copies of softback at $7.95 each   = $ _____

Please add $.50 postage and handling per book $ _____

                                    TOTAL $ _____

Name _____

Address _____

City, State _____ Zip _____

LIFE-CHANGING BOOKS
TO HELP YOU

YOU CAN OVERCOME: By far the most important preparation for Christians to make for the difficult days ahead is spiritual preparation. This book outlines from the Scriptures why it is essential to become a bondslave of God and how to be an overcomer to His glory.

BECOME LIKE JESUS: Most Christians would readily agree that we should become like Jesus. This book helps you understand from the Scriptures why we should try to become like Jesus and how to do so. We believe this book will revolutionize your life!

Dr. Carlton Booth, Retired Fuller Seminary Professor says:

"This book will once again stir with in the hearts of earnest Christians a desire to be conformed to the image of Jesus Christ."

Paul Hegstrom, Pastor, says:

"If I could only have two books in my library, they would be the Bible and BECOME LIKE JESUS."

Omega Publications   BC-241

P. O. Box 4130, Medford, OR 97501

$ _____ for _____ copies of *You Can Overcome* ($9.99)

_____ for _____ copies of *Become Like Jesus* ($9.99)

☐   Enclosed is $17 for *both* books.

(Price subject to change without notice.)

Name _____

Address _____

City, State _____ Zip _____

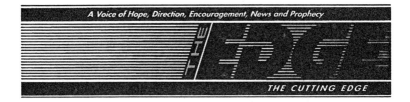
A Voice of Hope, Direction, Encouragement, News and Prophecy

THE CUTTING EDGE

The Cutting Edge is a monthly Christian publication offering a *voice of hope, direction, and encouragement in the midst of troubled times.* You will gain a reputable resource that strongly advocates godly Christian values and highly esteems marriage and family, providing aids for healthier, happier relationships. This one-source, timely digest is *a watchman for you, alerting* you to items you might not otherwise see that pertain to you. That includes relevant news updates on world conditions and the church worldwide; key articles by Christian leaders that equip the saints for the work of the ministry (Ephesians 4:11-13), current perspectives on prophecy; articles to help you prepare for tough times and emergencies; and ways you can strengthen your immune system and physical health.

Through all of our publications, tapes, and videos, as well as the speaking ministry of Jack & Jeani Harroun, we seek to help the body of Christ to mature into the fullness of Christ, to be prepared spiritually, emotionally, and physically for the challenging future we are facing.

- -

The Cutting Edge Ministries   (541)826-9877
Jack & Jeani Harroun   Orders: (800)343-1111
P.O. Box 1788   E-mail: Edge@the-cutting-edge.org
Medford, OR 97501   Website: the-cutting-edge.org

☐ Enclosed is a $25 contribution. Please send me a 1-year subscription to *The Cutting Edge* monthly newsmagazine at this special introductory rate (regularly $30; $65 U.S. airmail overseas; $45 U.S. to Canada).

☐ Please send information on other helpful books, audio tape albums, and videos.

Name _____

Address _____

City _____ State _____ Zip _____

ORDER FORM AND
INFORMATION REQUEST

Omega Publications   B4-101
P.O. Box 4130
Medford, OR 97501

$_____Please send me _____ copies of
The Incredible Cover-Up by Dave MacPherson ($8.99)

Please send me the following materials
by Dr. James McKeever:
(Prices subject to change without notice)

    ____ $_____ *The Rapture Book* ($9.99)
    ____ _____ *Revelation for Laymen* ($7.95)
    ____ _____ *You Can Overcome* ($9.99)
    ____ _____ *Become Like Jesus* ($9.99)
    ____ _____ *The Future Revealed* ($9.99)
    ____ _____ *Your Key to His Kingdom* ($9.99)

TOTAL AMOUNT ENCLOSED $ _____

Please send me more information about:

    ☐ *The Cutting Edge,* a monthly newsletter
    ☐ The helpful *Omega Deeper Life Minibooks*
    ☐ Other books distributed by Omega Publications
    ☐ Tapes and video tapes

Send the materials I have indicated to:

Name _____

Address _____

City, State _____ Zip _____